Dancing In The Rain

Dancing In The Rain

A Vibrant Young Woman Faces Cancer

KIMBERLY FOWLER

Dancing In The Rain

Published in the United States of America by Percepxion Media Corp.

Cover and Interior Design by Aaron Tinsley, Tinsley Design Studio.

Library of Congress Control Number: 2011936828

Fowler, Kimberly

Dancing In The Rain/A Vibrant Young Woman Faces Cancer

ISBN: 978-1-93-685800-2

1. Fowler, Kimberly. 2. Boxler, MaDeé. 3. Biography & Autobiography. 4. Personal Memoirs. 5. Cancer

---

This book is based on true life and is, in its essence, a work of historical reconstruction. Some names of hospital staff, patients and friends have been changed. Certain events dates and times may be inaccurate and some sequences may have been changed or altered purely by the author's design, motivated by the wish to advance the story line, serve the greater purpose of the book and protect the paths of those who knew MaDee. Any significant errors or omissions are purely unintentional.

The soul of a child is never about an illness.

~Unknown

Dedication

To the young and the young at heart, who face the ravages of a cancer diagnosis with bravery, fortitude and perseverance and to their tireless caretakers and the capable medical teams that so miraculously perform. To my young son, Evan, who received a cancer diagnosis at the age of seven. There was no greater purpose than to care for you, even while I was thinking you were the one who was taking care of me. To my eldest son, Ryan, for choosing the right path and people, when all about you was crumbling under the heavy weight of saving your brother's life. I can only hope to one day emulate your God-given wisdom. To the family of MaDeé Nicole Boxler, this book is for you. Thank you for allowing me to share your canvas and color the rainbow that is MaDeé.

May you always find feathers....

In Memoriam

MaDeé Nicole Boxler

(1987-2010)

Table of Contents

Foreword

This is the story of MaDee Boxler, who at the age of 20 years old was diagnosed with Hodgkin's lymphoma after severe pain in her stomach led to the discovery of a mass of abnormal lymph nodes in her chest. Just short of two years from her diagnosis, she died.

Fortunately, Hodgkin's lymphoma and all cancers in general are relatively rare diseases in children and young adults. According to National Cancer Institute statistics, Hodgkin's lymphoma is diagnosed annually in approximately 8,000 people in the United States, with 45% of cases occurring in people under the age of 35 years. Cure rates are actually "good" with approximately 80% of patients alive 5 years after their diagnosis. As a consequence, there are 170,000 people living in the United States after a diagnosis of Hodgkin's lymphoma.

As is true with cancer in general, we have not yet unraveled the mysteries of what causes Hodgkin's lymphoma, why it spreads in some patients and not in others, and why the same treatment may cure one patient, but not another. We do know that most patients with Hodgkin's lymphoma will be cured of their disease. We also know that with continued research and persistence, we will cure even more children and adults in the years ahead and in ways that hopefully leave them with less long-term complications of their treatment.

MaDee's story is an amazing one. I had the privilege of being a part of it and the honor to be one of her treating physicians. MaDee was an extremely vibrant young woman. Though it sounds like a cliché, MaDee's smile literally lit up an entire room. She had an incredible smile. She was able to smile and laugh through the worst of her disease and its treatment. Her story is one of strength and perseverance. There were very few, if any, visits in the 15 months that I knew MaDee where I had the chance to deliver really good news to her. Most of the time the news was, at best, "not worse." Despite this, MaDee remained positive and focused on both accomplishing the treatments we all hoped would make her better and at the same time living her life to the fullest. We always knew with MaDee exactly where we stood. We knew that she insisted that we honor her desire to fight cancer within the context of her living as full and as complete a life as possible. I believe that it was her strong desire to live and live well that contributed to her living as long as she did in the face of an unrelenting cancer.

MaDee's unremitting desire to fight fueled my desire to fight for her. Despite all the bad news, clinic visits, stays in the hospital for more treatment, and difficult phone calls, it was always a pleasure to see MaDee, and I was truly fortunate to have shared the time with her that I did. When she lost her hair, she did not cover her head but wore her baldness with pride. It was as if she declared to the world her cancer and her will not to let it affect her living her life. She knew that she was beautiful and the same person with and without it. She was able to brighten my days and those of everyone involved in her care, even if she did spray us and her chemo named targets with her Nerf gun from time to time. MaDee made friends wherever she was, both in the community and in the hospital.

MaDee's life was ultimately cut short by a brutal disease that she certainly did not bring on herself or in any way deserve. Unfortunately, MaDee's story is far from unique. More young adults and children will be diagnosed with cancer today and, like MaDee, they and their families will begin a journey they could not have imagined before that fateful day of diagnosis. Like MaDee, so many will be compelled to mature too quickly, as they are forced into a complex world of doctors, nurses, medicines, procedures, and hospitals that they can barely comprehend. Again and again, these children and young people will show a level of courage many of us will never be asked to exhibit. And over and over again, they will inspire us to fight with them, for their lives.

We are very fortunate that MaDee took the time and had the wherewithal in hospital beds, in waiting room chairs, and on her couch at home to document her journey while it was fresh and occurring. Her own writings serve as the basis of this story, filled in by her family and friends to fulfill a promise they made to her to finish the story she had begun to write but could not finish herself. The power of this book is that it is not a book where time has dulled the edges, but is instead a book containing the words of a young adult who walked amid the halls of an oncology ward and listened to the sounds no one wants to hear, including her own. MaDee's expression of raw emotions about her illness and its impact on her life is the mark of the story's excellence.

This book is valuable in that it focuses on the things many of us find difficult to deal with, especially under the duress of an unwanted and life changing diagnosis. This book is a valuable addition in the library of young adults facing cancer. It is an essential resource for the families of the newly diagnosed or the relapsed patient. It is a must read for physicians, nurses, laboratory technicians, social workers, pharmacists and all those who care for the ill and help them to live fully and well in the face of sickness.

It has been my honor and my distinct privilege to have been one of MaDee's treating physicians and to be asked to write these words at the beginning of her story.

Michael G. Douvas, M.D.
Assistant Professor of Medicine, Hematology and Oncology
University of Virginia School of Medicine
Charlottesville, Virginia

Acknowledgments

Things happen very quickly when a cancer diagnosis is received. When the fateful words from a doctor hit the air, every ounce of your being and that of those in your orbit is immediately required to react, in a minute, and often, on a dime. Cancer rocks and spins the gravitational rotation of life, as you once knew it. Never satisfied, once cancer enters the arena, the beast begins to chew pieces and parts of you up, then spats the undigested portions back out at you again. In the next instant, *it* comes lunging back, biting for more. There is no time for thinking, much less *thanking*, the scores of people who rally by your side, in every conceivable and imaginable way possible. Each thought, word and deed, beyond the words, "It's cancer," is focused, and rightfully so, on preserving life.

Because MaDee never had the chance to say good-bye in proper fashion, I believe that she would rest easier if I made commemorative mention of the people who so remarkably touched her life and that of her loved ones throughout the crisis known as life-threatening disease. She would want me to honor those who blessed and graced her world and those individuals that she considered herself privileged to love.

During the writing of this book, I made a concerted effort to squeeze from MaDee's journals and the hundreds of stories that I was privileged to hear, every ounce of gratitude embedded in her world and in her words and place them here, in gracious acknowledgment, for the selfless acts and the love bestowed upon her. Until the publication of my next book, it is my hope, as the author of this memoir, that the individuals completely deserving of *my* humble gratitude will understand and be content to wait for recompense.

When MaDee entered the gates of Heaven, I believe that she gave *all* the glory to God. MaDee would want us to know that from her living, she grew in large strides towards thankfulness and grace. MaDee was most humbled by her lessons in service and what it meant to love a living, loving and forgiving God. She was *awestruck* by the idea of perfect healing.

Thank you to Tamara Talley-Campbell. Mom. MaDee knew just how strong you were, Tamara, and she knew, as well, that she took absolutely every single thing out on you. She lashed out at you because you were the single person, besides Abby, that was *brave enough* to always be with her. MaDee knew that you could take it, especially when she could not. Even though MaDee chided you for crying, she felt the same sadness and yearned for the same things that you wished for her.

MaDee wanted you to know, Tamara, in no uncertain terms, that what you did for her as her caregiver, and as her mother, meant *more than a great deal* to her. MaDee recognized that you had her cancer, too and really, you still have it, caught up in the memory of losing her. While MaDee is healed of her pain, your healing is still in the future, when you finally meet up with her again. She really did consider it her fault, Tamara, every moment that she couldn't or wouldn't acknowledge your advice, love and support. Thank you for recognizing that she was really just a scared little girl and very new in her walk of faith; thank you also for honoring her true love and all the special dreams she held close to her heart—the kind of happiness that you have found with Steve.

Tamara, it takes a special mom to know how to absorb the shock waves of a daughter screaming, "*Don't touch me, Mom,*" only to have her then say, "*...but don't you dare let me fall.*" You were the best momma a girl like MaDee could ever have. You must always remember, Tamara, that God handpicked you for MaDee and Abby, and He made you, in His likeness, *specifically* for loving them, like you have done, *TTT,* and all. You have made MaDee's love light forever shine and you are a wonderful grandma, who deserves every happiness.

To MaDee's physicians. The tasks you have undertaken, especially in the fields of Hematology and Oncology are noble. To the astounding and intelligent men and women, who come to work every day to treat and care for so many, like MaDee, in each exam room and hospital bed across our great nation, thank you. To the researchers, technicians, nurses, aides, clerical staff, cafeteria workers and janitorial staff, MaDee knew that each of you, in your own way, were doing absolutely everything you could do to care for her, just by coming to work. Those persons who sat beside MaDee in the hospitals and in the exam rooms knew the great tasks that were performed, by each and every one of you. But, what some of us may not have known, is that MaDee required *more* from her health care team and that each of you *delivered.* MaDee insisted that her providers honor her wish that cancer come in a close second to the idea of her living well, which always took first prize. While she let you do your jobs, you in turn, allowed her to do hers, which was to live with a grace and a zest for life, undeterred by disease. Thank you for treating, with wisdom, patience and understanding, the *whole* of MaDee.

To Tom Boxler. Dad. MaDee always needed you; every girl needs their daddy. She would definitely want to thank you for the times that you stood by her, at the tool bench and at the hospital. She spent her whole life trying to get closer to you and to understand you. The fact that you were with her, in the end, was meaningful and touched her heart.

To Nan and Pop. MaDee loved having two moms at certain times and you fit that bill perfectly, Nannie. *My* how she worshiped her hero, Pop. Thank you, Nan, for diffusing her hot little bossy *punkin'* head so many times over the years and for *always* thinking to put ribbons in her hair. Thank you for opening your door to her and loving on her in the special way that only grandparents can. Your love (and your coffee) made MaDee, MaDee, and we can easily surmise that nothing could compare with the joy she felt when she ran to greet Pop, in Heaven. She is taking *very good* care of him, of that we can rest assured.

To Abby. Where do we begin? MaDee's story, for the most part, is your story, Abby. To call you her *sister* will never be enough. To compliment you as her *best friend,* is a gargantuan understatement. To describe the two of you as *soul mates* comes slightly closer. To paint you as the *axis* of MaDee's orbit is probably getting nearer to the galaxy that was the mark and pinion of your love for one another.

I think MaDee knew all along how this was going to go, don't you, Abby? Wasn't it just like her to protect you? I think she planned every step along the way to prepare you for her passing, but, then, she simply couldn't fathom leaving you. It would have made her cry and we all know how she did not want anyone or anything to *ever* make her cry. Her love for you, Abby, was too wide and too great and far too deep to even think of leaving you. When MaDee glanced briefly at the chasm that would come of losing you, she practically *willed* that she be allowed to take a part of you with her, to Heaven. That is where you have always fit best, Abby, and where you will always belong: inside her spirited soul. Anything less than this connection would be tantamount to complete and total devastation, and we all know that MaDee would have *none* of that for you. Please know as well, Abby, that you are indeed one of the lucky ones; you have been gifted with a chance to have loved in the best and most complete way possible, this side of Heaven. MaDee continues to watch over you, Cy, and Juddy, always and forever. She loved you best, Abby. It's just as simple as that.

To Uncle Charlie. Thanks for *always* being there for MaDee and more, for knowing exactly what she needed, even before she knew that she needed it. Your talks kept MaDee going. There was nothing like a good cry on your shoulder, time at the range with you, or simply *vegging* in front of the TV next to you.

To Aunt Sara. The greatest gift, sometimes, is in *not* being mothered. Your recognition of this need in MaDee was what allowed her to finally find the space she desperately needed to think. Thank you for allowing her to be alone with her thoughts.

To Lil' Cuz. Brittany. Cherished. Angel MaDee is always watching and always listening; never forget that.

Grandma and Grandpap. Your prayers and uplifting words on the CaringBridge site rang as true as the bells heard at Mass. We must bottle your homemade cinnamon rolls.

To The First Young Man She Truly Loved. You were very important to our MaDee...you always were and you always will be. We all know who you are, just as you know who you are and honestly we would all be smarter, too, if we acknowledged your love for MaDee, forever. You must know, that MaDee never wanted to cause you any pain, or give you any grief, and she took full responsibility for those times when the cancer got the better of her loving ways. MaDee would have been mad, too, if the tables were turned. Because MaDee was sick, and for no other reason, she had to leave you, but she couldn't help it and she always wanted to gift you with nothing but the best. You loved a great and strong woman and she loved you right back. You taught her about love and loss and the realities of relationship through *the hard stuff.* Do her proud. Make her happy. Honor her memory. Remember her smile. Live and love like MaDee did.

To Amanda. To think that at such a young age you fought so tirelessly alongside MaDee, after all that you had been through, and against such terrific odds, did not go unnoticed for a second and speaks volumes about your character and the depth of your compassion. For every single minute that you stood by MaDee, she noticed and she was truly grateful.

To Hayley. Never stop believing that you can do this. If MaDee was a hero, then you are a titan. Thanks for showing MaDee how to boss those nurses, baby girl. MaDee loves you and all the little children in the hospital beds beside you. *Shine.*

To Lacey and to Jena. Thank you, for *always* being there....

To R. I think that MaDee would look down now on you with such supreme fondness, for what could have been and for your grand and perfect entrance into her life at just about the perfectly wrong time. *Ahhh*, you are going to make someone the luckiest woman in the world. You must believe that. MaDee did.

To *The Boys.* Dom. Tamara just might have been right—maybe one should marry their best friend. Thank you for *fixin' it*, making MaDee laugh and letting her lean on your strong shoulders. CJ, you were her *puppy love*, her *CJ bear* and the most fun a girl could ever have. And to *The Pack*—Ryan, Zach and Lee—thanks for always eating her cookies and for including her, in everything. Make sure she would *approve.*

To Lynne. You are the *pillar* of what it means to be gracious and giving. There is never going to be another one like you and MaDee and her family have always known that there will not be a way to thank you completely for your boundless spirit and for your incredible love. Your friendship, support and tireless efforts in seeing to it that MaDee's legacy lives on, and that The MaDee Project and her story remain fresh in the minds of so many is the subject of daily and humble gratitude. Lynne, may you reap, ten thousand fold, in reward, what you have so generously sown.

To Pastor Jeff and Teri. Inspiration. Guidance. Support. Understanding. Thank you for illuminating MaDee's walk. May you continue to bless and touch the lives of others in the same selfless ways.

To Mary C. You saved MaDee's life and she felt immense gratitude.

To Kerri and to Brooke. The epitome of what is best and of great friendship. Devoted. Simply devoted.

To Mo. Momma misses you.

To Cy. *Heaven sent.*

To Juddy. Jeff. You are a good man, a wonderful husband and a great Daddy. *Teach him in thy ways* and treat her like a lady. Always. She may seem tough, but she is definitely *all* worth it. MaDee would tell you so.

Thank you to the residents, staff and volunteers at Bethany Hall. While it may have seemed as if MaDee was helping you, really, you were helping her—to reconnect and to forget *her* disease, if only for a day. Working with women suffering from addiction and helping young adults to reclaim their lives, from what many would consider the realm of *lost causes,* was the marker and pinion of MaDee's very existence. MaDee was profoundly touched by the spirit of your remarkable mission. The long hours at Bethany Hall required that MaDee give up the cancer experience and simply, hang out, doing what she did best. There was no better medicine than the *hope of love*, even if there were no guarantees. *Thy Kingdom come*, indeed.

To the facility, staff and coaches at Roanoke College. Thank you for profoundly touching the spirit of MaDee with your support and strenuous efforts to assist her in completing her degree requirements, while undergoing intense chemo. Although most of the lessons MaDee learned were not found in any of your textbooks, the students and those within your hallowed hallways that surrounded MaDee in loving camaraderie and prayer, speak volumes about the high caliber of your institution.

Thank you to the readers of MaDee's CaringBridge page, and to the hundreds of supporters in the communities of Staunton, Waynesboro, and Roanoke, Virginia and to the people in Augusta and Highland counties of the great State of Virginia and beyond. Your outpouring of love, generosity and prayer lifted heavy spirits. So many times we as followers feel that our words are *simply inadequate* on the CaringBridge and CarePage websites that are set up for those coping with illness. We hesitate to write. But, these words did *not* ever fail MaDee. They were like oxygen and moved through her and her family as only spirited, crisp white sails on deep blue ocean waters can do. MaDee was blessed to be beneath the winds of your generosity and your prayers.

And finally, from MaDee, to all of the sick, the lonely, the tired, the recovering, the suffering and the grieving—to any one of you reading—that feel the tremendous emptiness or despair of another day, please know that MaDee would consider the act of putting your feet on the carpeted floor and rising from your bed, willing to take things one day at a time, to be heroic, in and of itself. As MaDee always said, "Continue to pray."

MaDee

Introduction

For MaDee it was pancakes and a parade; for me, it was scrambled eggs and school. Two years before MaDee was diagnosed with cancer, my son Evan, was diagnosed with leukemia. We spent the next four years fighting cancer together. I sat with him when he could not sleep; I slept beside him when he could. I carried him when he could not walk and I bought him a cane when he could. Evan was just seven years old when he was diagnosed and his treatment would encapsulate over one-half of his young, short and innocent life. I watched my young warrior as he battled a beast so formidable as to bend, twist and shake, to the core, every single belief system we possessed and every single plan that we had ever made.

My life became that of his sole caretaker, twenty four hours a day, 365 days a year. Many of the days I spent battling cancer beside my son were without sleep and in the throes of witnessing a pain in him and such a debilitating disease process that he required treatments that could only be described as unrelenting, at their weakest. A vast majority of my time was spent away from my eldest son, while Evan and I were in isolation, at Clinic, in hospital rooms or traveling to and from the next appointment for the chemotherapy that would cure him. All of these experiences required a medical expertise typically reserved for Residents and Fellows on a Hematology-Oncology rotation, at a large medical teaching institution.

The hopes and dreams that I held for myself and my astonishing two sons, were put completely on hold, as I did what I could do to bolster my youngest boy as he attempted to slay a formidable, dastardly dragon without the aid of swords. Cancer taught me that unlike in an enchanted forest, in the world of disease, the good guy doesn't always win.

But, what cancer did not know, is that it left in my belly a fire as strong as any frothing from inside the mouth of the beast. It made me care for my sick son in the only way I knew how, with great love and greater determination and the type of devotion only a parent facing life-threatening circumstances can possess. If I could have loved Evan to healthy, I would have done just that. A parent of a child with cancer loves greatly, but, at the same time, feels the fear and the constant poke from the monster. In between the insurance, the medical jargon, the video games and the ready smiles, meant to gladden the heart of my child, I was, as a cancer parent, in constant and ready position to dare and defy the creature to come any closer. But, sometimes, cancer does not listen, and it advances, rapidly and unceasingly, despite the best of intentions.

As my son came to the end of his years of chemotherapy, my sister, Lynne wrote to me with the news that someone near and dear to her heart had just met the selfsame dragon. I began following MaDee's journey. I prayed for her and I rejoiced when the news was good; I cried when it was not. I came to know and love MaDee. With each piece of news about her, I could feel the roll of my stomach, and knew her caretakers, especially her mom and her sister, might be feeling it, too. I knew, to the point of gagging, the smells of the treatments MaDee was receiving. I walked similar hallways in the cancer wards she was finding herself in. I saw far too many small patients, like MaDee did, within every partially closed door and dimly lit hospital room—each with a story of their own to tell—and many people who loved them by the beds.

I understood that the painful procedures MaDee merely mentioned were not sparing her the details. I instinctively added up the effects of the drugs she was being given and the toll these were likely taking on her, and hopefully, on her cure rates, and what is more, I noticed that remarkably, MaDee never even mentioned that some of her treatments fell on her birthday, many were just before her beloved sister's wedding, each of them interfered with her relationships and all of them caused her to struggle to keep up in school. It was only when I read her private journals did I discover what I thought in fact had to have been true.

Because I had experienced cancer as a parent, I knew what certain chemo looked like and from the descriptions of my son and the nurses, what it felt like going into the shrunken veins and ports of children. The nurses on a pediatric oncology floor leave nothing to surprise, so that small children might overcome their fear and know what to expect. I had been there, next to the beds. I had watched and held my child during many of the same procedures. I paid special attention to the nurses, and to the things my son told me, such that each time MaDee spoke of her unrelenting nausea and extreme fatigue, I could literally have held the barf bin for her...as I talked to an insurance representative on the phone...feel her begin to doze...reaching to check her temperature...while eating half of a stale peanut butter sandwich...in three day old jeans. This process is the *family* that cancer creates.

I knew what MaDee's scans and lumbar punctures entailed, without anesthesia, with contrast and without, and I knew she was *tougher than nails* to have laid and watched on the table, as she sometimes did, even on days when she had a school term paper due. I knew how dangerous a low blood count was for MaDee and how often she teetered on the edge of admissions, but chose instead to shop, just daring her precarious counts to fall enough to stop her.

I also knew what it felt like for MaDee's mom, Tamara, to lie in a single parent's bed, of a dark and cold night, and listen to her child's wishes; not wishes for princes and coaches, but wishes from her girl for just one minute of relief; wishes to know that God really was there with her, amid pleas that He might come to help her with the pain. I knew how it was to hold a child ravaged by disease and to slumber with them beside me, at night, so that thcy would feel safe and so that they *would* be safe. I knew what it was to have absolutely no control over the reports from the doctors, which many times, for MaDee, were horrific. I have dealt with cancer for years and years and years and I knew the same path was, unfortunately, being paved, brick by brick, for MaDee and her family.

I wrote often to MaDee with my thoughts. I knew what sort of energy her mother might be generating and the likely tone of her despondent prayers. I found that I could compare her sister

Abby's strong, steadfast and undying love for MaDee, to that I felt for my sons. I knew to the depth of my soul that Abby, who was recently married, was literally performing, like a blind tight-rope walker at a circus, thrust into a world, with no training and no nets beneath her, no road map to guide her, as she cared for her sister and watched her lifeblood pour into the best friend and sole confidant that she had ever known. I knew that for Abby, the act of seeing her protector, her hero, her kindred spirit and her only sibling fading, right before her eyes, was the stuff of which unrelenting nightmares were made. And, as I heard about Abby watching MaDee slip further and further away from her clutches and from this earth, I knew that Abby was going to have to do the unthinkable. She was going to have to release her and there was absolutely nothing I was going to be able to do to erase the emptiness or ease her pain.

Evan finished his treatments. Slowly, I began to raise myself up and climb to the top of the rabbit hole that was cancer's long and arduous gully, called active treatment. Evan and I soon washed up on the shores of life A/C or *after cancer.* It was then that I had the presence of mind and enough rest to follow MaDee's story, more closely. I have always believed that there are few, if any, coincidences in this life. The link between MaDee's story and my emergence from the depths of the treatment world was beginning to create in my mind the idea that MaDee was becoming a sort of catalyst and that her lessons would bring comfort to me. In certain unmistakable ways, this young woman and I were going to be a part of a spectacular and universal story, together.

There are many young people fighting cancer, like MaDee and like Evan. More are diagnosed each and every day. So many kids are waging war and there are far too many precious young that are leaving us, entirely too soon. It is heartbreakingly common for earthly healing to fail. I knew that I had to see to it that the stories of these young people were not lost. I knew that I had to know more, about MaDee.

I can remember days, when I stood, with telephone in hand, as my son's aunt and MaDee's close family friend grew in her knowledge of the barbarian attacking her friend. I listened for hours as she shared with me the intimate details that MaDee and her family were experiencing. Because I was one who had fought in similar hospital trenches, it was her fervent hope that I could do *something*—anything—to bring solace, during an inconsolable time.

Sometimes I would ask questions and inquire about the settings on the machines hooked up to MaDee. At other times, I would simply ask, *how does she look?* Sometimes, I would know what to pray for; many times, I did not. MaDee and her family, just like me and my boys, were in the middle of a fight for their precious girl's life and they were facing, like so many do, insurmountable odds.

Before MaDee left us and while she was in the throngs of relapse, she came up with an idea. MaDee made a decision to tell her story. Sitting in a hospital bed one night, she devised a plan and sometime later, she told her mom about it. One can almost surmise that MaDee knew what was to come when she asked her Mom to see to it that her message was shared. You see, MaDee never stopped thinking. She was a planner and she knew the steps that were necessary to see her goals to fruition. This young adult was the *go to girl*; the one who might just have written the book on maturity and futures, had she survived. MaDee spent great expanses of her short life geared towards helping others—friend, family member and stranger—alike. MaDee wanted her dream and her work helping others to continue. She therefore had the foresight, even in the midst of grueling treatments, to begin to write parts of her story, in journal fashion, in the off chance and with the idea that she might help others, facing similar diseases. Tamara and Abby promised MaDee that if she could not complete her work, that they would see to it that it was written.

Uncanny happened next, amidst the sadness and the grief. A few short months later, at her funeral, MaDee was described by her pastor as a woman who had touched the lives of many, with a wonderful *story* to share. This same pastor literally walked over to the family, seated in the front row and handed out writing pens to those who loved her best. These pens, he explained, were so that MaDee's story would be told, and that her memory and her message would live on.

I simply borrowed their pens.

A few short months later, I set about on a nearly one year journey to discover this remarkable young woman. While MaDee's family and her friends continued to deal with life without her, I gathered and I painted a picture in my mind and in scores of blank notebooks. I compiled voluminous testimonies, journals, calls, interviews, emails, texts, CaringBridge pages, Facebook entries, baby books, old letters, mementos, cards and I asked a thousand and one questions that were gently placed before the family. There were personal interviews and transcripts of conversations with those closest to MaDee; many of whom shared their innermost feelings and heartfelt memories of her. It was the gathering of the stories from those who loved her best that filled the pages that I was writing. While MaDee lived only twenty-two years, she lived them fully and she lived them completely and the directions she left for me were quite clear.

What I was able to patch together and sew up, was the story MaDee began telling when she wrote pieces and parts of it, and put it aside—for tomorrow—in much the same way we work on a jigsaw puzzle, one piece at a time and over hours. I started with the outside perimeter of the frame and then I held each and every nugget of MaDee's life up to the light for further reflection; I studied it, turned it round and round, thought about its placement, its color and, finally, when I was completely comfortable, I set it in its proper position, within the storybook pages that housed her. What emerged was *Dancing in the Rain.*

I want to make it perfectly clear that I did not write this book alone. Like a rainbow that looks over a city in ruins, I colored it, one color at a time, with an endearing woman, named MaDee, guiding my pen and teaching me. Also, I must confess, that in the writing of her memoir, I felt compelled to address the notion that *had MaDee lived,* there were things she surely *would have said* and I, therefore, took liberties. With painstaking care and prayer, laced with empathy, compassion and pieces of my imagination, I attempted to *say them for her*, based on all that I had come to know and read about her. I attempted to pencil in the words she might have spoken, had she had the time. I did some reading between the lines of each and every message, each word written to her and everything that could be remembered. I knew in no uncertain terms, from every message that MaDee left, that she would definitely want certain things said and that there should be no omissions; I had no doubt about that, at all. Any assumptions this creates in the reader, or any erroneous tidbits of story are entirely mine and I take full and complete responsibility for them—in the only way that I know how—as a mom, a Christian, a cancer caregiver and, as the author.

MaDee was a living testament to the notion that there is *always tomorrow*. But, tomorrow, MaDee would learn, was not always going to turn out as one would expect. In her case and in mine, the living through of the yesterdays was not at all what it was cracked up to be, or anything like we would have *wanted* it to be. While tomorrow always comes, many times it arrives in despicable black paper, all tied up with the strings of sadness; its contents overflowing with loss. Further, finding oneself in the throngs of a future day without the ones we love, is *beyond hard*. MaDee was such an old soul to have recognized these notions and by doing so, she chiseled out an opportunity to speak a clear message within the pages of this book.

MaDee spent her entire life wearing ribbons in her hair, until chemotherapy took her hair. MaDee spent her whole life loving others, until she could not see or speak to hold anyone, any more. MaDee spent her days dancing, in those crazy-colored boots or with whimsical flip flops on her feet, even in the rain, until they covered her toes in blankets. Cancer took away her tomorrows. But, MaDee hung steadfast to the belief that *today* is, in fact, where the lesson resides; today is right where we belong, even as we suffer or miss our loved ones.

MaDee learned that life is not all about dodging the raindrops, as the old saying goes; it is more about learning to dance in the rain...and over the boulders and in the muddy puddles and through the darkest of the storms. *My, how she could dance.* MaDee brought to each season, a little two-step, entirely of her own creation. MaDee learned, often in spite of herself, that there is, in each of us, a season and a time...for everything.

Writing this book for the family was renewing. Authoring MaDee's story for her loved ones has taught me that, contrary to any storm a cancer diagnosis might bring, in me was an *invincible summer.* I hope that the message of MaDee will touch the lives of all who read it.

KIMBERLY FOWLER

Valencia, California
September, 2011

Chapter One

Like A Carolina Sandhill Peach

MaDee never knew a gray hair. Tamara considered this thought, briefly, but quickly dismissed it and rather shuddered at the notion that she had even allowed it to enter the room. She looked down and spread the fingers of her left hand and began to pull at the green latex glove with an upwards snap of each finger and on her right, she remembered to roll the ends up and over the top, as she had seen the nurses do. She tossed the set towards the trash basin, and watched as one landed over the edge of the hot water spigot, near the lip of the sink. She would tend to that in a bit.

MaDee's face looked beaded now and Tamara stood up to see about wiping the small drops of fluid from the bridge of her nose. She noticed the furrow then and gave it an upwards whisk of her thumb, twice, like she was wiping ketchup from MaDee's face. Reaching behind her with her bare hand, she found the half open metal drawer next to the bed and she reached for the tissues that she knew were inside. She pinched a batch up into her fingers, because she knew that she would need more to compare with those she used at home. She wondered, briefly, if she should place a Bible in the drawer so that the next person would see more inside than one single-use alcohol wipe, a forgotten Dora the Explorer Band-Aid in a baggie and a thin silver packet of Vaseline.

A bit of the protective eye gel had slipped below MaDee's closed eyelids. The gel kept her deep brown eyes moist and Tamara knew that she needed this. *MaDee never cried much, as a baby, and certainly not growing up.* It seemed that nothing could ever make MaDee cry. Tamara wondered if the nurse had added the gel to MaDee's eyes so that she would not *have* to cry. Or, was it there because the staff had heard that both of her girls chided *her* for weeping too freely? *I've never figured all that out.* It was just one more thing that Tamara knew her girls shared, strictly between them.

Tamara stroked the fine peach fuzz that was beginning to grow back on MaDee's perfectly shaped head. She wished that she could loosen the tape across her cheeks; but *it holds the ventilator tube steady,* she remembered, on a machine that breathed life into the most unlikely of persons to ever need such a thing. She sat back down in the brown leatherette chair and looked again at the underside of her daughter's face. *What act could it be of modern medicine that allows the chemo to destroy you and then lets you grow such fine, baby soft hair again, so soon?* She leaned forward in the bedside recliner chair that had now caused the back of her beige blouse to stick, as she moved her ear down towards her shoulder and placed her hand on the curve of her waist. She rubbed. *Standing might be better* and she walked over to the shelf for another set of gloves from the box, but then she placed them beside the blanket. *MaDee liked her cheeks rubbed, round and round in small circular motions, as if polishing a delicate silver spoon.* She could not do that in gloves. Touching her again, now, *it certainly seemed a face as soft as a baby's, and, filled with too much fluid, it looked just as round.*

MaDee's wires and lines seemed to be going and coming in the most orchestrated, yet random of directions, like a New York subway map and that made it difficult to know where to touch her, except her face, her feet and the top of her thick woolen cover. Tamara just *knew* that MaDee would soon wake up and feel better, and that she would want her nails shaped and painted, immediately. Tamara hoped the nurses here in the Medical Intensive Care Unit knew how much thought MaDee always put into looking her best. She hoped that they would understand that as soon as she could, MaDee would want to have the bed raised so that she could sit up. She would hug her knees up to her chest, wrap her arms around them and then sleepily glance down at her toes, insisting that she needed a pedicure for her pretty pink flip flops, the ones she had packed and had planned to wear on her feet during walks around the grounds.

Tamara always loved watching the way MaDee would paint each nail, arch her feet towards her and stretch her toes apart, as if they were the fingers of a small child reaching for the key of G, on the piano. She would look down as she spoke, at her toes, likely just imagining all the places her feet could take her. Tamara wondered if she had remembered to bring MaDee's OPI *I'm Not Really A Waitress* bright red nail polish from the room downstairs and now, she reached in to the drawer to make sure that it was there. She rubbed another inch of MaDee's top blanket, and then leaned close to the side of her face. "Baby girl," she whispered, "I just knew I should have held you more."

Abby, who was sitting quietly in MaDee's cubicle, on the other side of the bed, never thought to respond when Mom talked like this; she had heard it all before. Abby brought only her eyes up and watched, as Mom turned to pick at the miniscule black remnant of mascara in the corner of her eye and swallowed deeply. Abby knew the lump in her throat had formed again. *These lumps have become like food.* Neither of them had been hungry, even though they had not eaten since yesterday.

Tamara took off her light beige summer sweater, meant for wearing under jackets, and set it over the safety rails that were tucked under the one large plastic covered mattress on the bed frame, as if to have it ready to offer to MaDee, should she need it. MaDee's shoulder was *so cold* to the touch that it made Tamara want to readjust an inch or so of the sheepskin covering her. Sitting back down, Tamara readjusted her glasses instead and smoothed the front of her wrinkled silk ruffled blouse. She began to read, looking up occasionally over the tortoise rims of her glasses. She looked at MaDee sometimes as if she had just spotted a neighbor over the brick fences that separate houses.

It was difficult to concentrate on reading a card that had arrived or anything else she might have brought in her bag to pick up, because the memories she had of MaDee came to her now, like heart-shaped river rocks spill water down a cool mountain stream. Every time she thought she had herself ready to turn the page, a monitor would sound or a red light would flash and a nurse would be quickly by MaDee's side, stealing the calmness from everyone. The alarms hooked up to her daughter scared Tamara more than the sound of a fire truck's siren at night. Things would grow unsteady until the nurse readjusted the settings which put MaDee, and the others, back to normal. Tamara so appreciated when they touched MaDee gently and more, when the staff taking care of her took the time to speak to her, as if she mattered as much as she did.

The flurry over MaDee was too often now and *certainly not a good time to talk*, very much like the rise and fall of the cadences in church music, the kinds of sounds that made a little boy want to whisper between stanzas. Thinking of church now and the sounds of the children as they sang of a Sunday, reminded Tamara that the same cherubic hymn was playing softly on the CD player that was turned on in the room. It was important that MaDee had something to listen to, the aide had said, even though Tamara had forgotten to hear it for the better part of the day. She did sometimes notice though, that the actions of the nurses were often in sync to the music—sharp and staccato—as if the song playing in the room had caused them to flip bandages and snap lines more quickly. At other times those taking care of MaDee treated her like ornate and delicate hand bells that ought not to be disturbed before their time. Tamara liked it when they washed MaDee down or gently pulled the covers away to check her skin and nail beds for color. When they spoke to MaDee in melodic tones, Tamara was sure they heard the sounds of the angels that were there in the room with them.

The click of the CD player made her look up at the clock. "Thank you," Tamara called out to the back of the door, as the nurse left the room and she chided herself for forgetting, again. Another forty eight minutes had come and gone and all she had done was compare the rapid, deep thumping of her heartbeat to that of MaDee's which pattered like rain on a window pane, through the machine's speaker. Sometimes, her heart and MaDee's beat as one; but most often they did not.

When Tamara was certain that no one was going to react to another variation and movement in MaDee's breath, she tried, again, to quiet the sigh intent on escaping her lips by closing them tightly, but she did not look away; the only time she could do that, and leave the staff to do their work, was when she was *sure* that MaDee was fine. Most days started, passed and ended in much the same way and little else got done, save for the task of watching MaDee for signs of wellness and tossing green gloves from the sink, into the trash.

The only thing that seemed to change with some regularity were the families that were crying and then leaving—walking down the hallway—alone. It was almost harder to sit in the waiting room and witness all of that emotion, than it was to be inside the glass-walled unit watching MaDee in the bed in the center of the room. Things were a different sort of quiet inside MICU; there was order and control and MaDee would appreciate that, in contrast to the drama playing out in the waiting rooms and hallways. The chaos, conversations, calls and unchecked crying could sometimes be heard in the room, even with the door closed and this would not sit well with MaDee. It was at those times that Tamara always remembered to turn up the music and hope that MaDee was listening to it.

The cotton swish of scrub suits as the nurses came into and out of the room, changed colors more rapidly now, like a child's kaleidoscope turned towards the sun. The air would move in the room, simply from the opening of the door and Tamara knew that the smell of clean linen mixed with lilac, like those in the scented warmers in the Airwick diffusers at home, would mean a new shift had started. The nurses were so good at what they did, as they covered their long shifts and cared for MaDee's quiet and sleeping body. Tamara always knew when it was time to eat, take a short walk, or ready herself to leave for the night by following their lead; but, she also knew when it was time *not* to leave.

It was nearing six o'clock in the evening and that was the time when the doctor would come in and have the words of her daughter's progress in his voice. Once in the morning and once in the evening. Rounds. Tamara *always* stayed in the room beside MaDee and waited for Rounds, wondering which doctor would come in to see them. There were some that she preferred seeing, over the rest, but only because they talked in terms she could understand and said words that made her believe the things she had been thinking. *Things were looking okay. MaDee will pull through this.*

"It has been such a long twenty-five months, dealing with all of this, hasn't it baby girl?" Tamara spoke, as if in prayer, over MaDee. Then, almost as if to ward off the thoughts of the last two years, in case MaDee was thinking about them too, and to insist that they all remain focused on the goal of complete healing, she leaned closer and began to *primp* MaDee for the doctor's visit. MaDee would want her to do that. She stroked MaDee's face, repositioned a jagged red plastic-coated wire and leaned closer to her daughter's right ear. "MaDee, the drug will be here, soon. You just keep on doing what you are doing," she said, as she met the next thought in her mind, which was to remember to ask how to spell the name of the medicine.

Tamara prayed and talked to MaDee more busily now as if pushing her prayers and her baby in a carriage, straight up a very tall hill. She dared not stop. She could not have cared less what anyone else thought or heard while she was next to her girl and speaking to her and she rarely acknowledged the nurses when they found her talking to MaDee or standing motionless in the room, staring at the air, with her palms cupping the side of her face, or crossing her breast. Tamara vowed to watch over MaDee and wait for any change, for as long as it took. She clung to the belief that she would know the moment when they had all turned the corner. Now, as the door opened and the doctor poked his head in, but then turned it back around just as quickly, Tamara looked at her sleeping daughter and sounded a prayer, in the voice of a mother who meant it.

God will heal you, MaDee.

Chapter Two

Someone To Lay Beside Me

MaDee no doubt heard her mom pray, at least a thousand times a day; Tamara was just sure of it, and she at least hoped, in the other times, that it was her prayers and the sound of their voices that MaDee listened to. *What if she just laid there and listened to the ticking of the minutes, one by one?* Tamara wasn't certain exactly what MaDee could hear, but she did want her to catch the atmosphere changing in the room, each time the monitors showed improvement.

In fact, according to the doctor that had spoken to Tamara last evening, and those who had been in the room the following day, "...there had been no further deterioration and progress was being measured in baby steps." The medicine that was meant to help save MaDee's liver was now on board and it was going to be a matter of keeping MaDee stable and steady, just waiting to see when her world would change and if her miracle would come.

MaDee's grimace would increase from time to time and Tamara could tell that MaDee liked the way some nurses touched her more than others. Each nurse was different; some poked harder than others. Some had soothing voices and some were far too loud. Moreover, MaDee had told Tamara time and again through treatment, that she could *literally* feel the different medicines going into her veins; the push-pull of the nurses and the infusions were distinct now. Tamara had some doubts about whether MaDee would recognize the pressure of the family's thoughts and prayers covering her and willing her to heal, like humidity coats a hot mid-eastern summer day, but she prayed that was the case.

When Tamara spoke to the Lord, she made a habit of bowing her head and pressing her hands more tightly on MaDee, as if touching her like that would keep her from leaving. After her Amen, Tamara patted MaDee's blankets, the way a seasoned mommy presses and burps a baby's back. Now that the staff had gone on to other things, MaDee looked *peaceful*, to Tamara, as if there was a difference between her sleeping and her being put to sleep.

Tamara knew that MaDee could at least hear them, when she listened, but it was important for her to relax and let the machine breathe for her. The drugs they were giving MaDee were strong but, even still, her vitals signified change on the monitors when the doctors came in and examined her. Tamara knew that MaDee trusted them, and that she would recognize their hands on her, making the task of doing nothing, easier. Tamara reminded her sleeping girl that she looked as if she might just be resting to those who didn't know, as she laid under the blankets, far away from anything that felt like home.

MaDee's body was wrapped warmly and bundled, like one might wrap a baby in a papoose or a warm flour tortilla over its chicken. The band of white tape across her face was too tight though, much like the orthodontic braces her young friends had worn to school, and everything smelled like *white, hospital and alcohol*, the kinds found in cupboards for skinned knees.

Tamara remarked to Abby that if they were to pick MaDee up, she would likely spew sea water. She looked swollen, like the inside of a white ocean conch shell at the shoreline. Tamara prayed that

MaDee might be dreaming of lighter places, like her favorite spot on the beach, or being in her bed with her dog, Mo. She noticed that there were minutes when MaDee looked as if she just might have found her way.

Abby stood to look. MaDee's baby soft bald head, devoid of her curly chocolate brown hair, was covered in her favorite maroon college cap. It felt soft and warm with MaDee in it, as Abby adjusted it now. Wondering if MaDee knew that it was not Mom touching her, she pressed her cheek against MaDee. "It's me, MaDee. Abby now." MaDee needed to smell her scent and recall it.

To Abby, MaDee appeared to be resting comfortably on the clean linens and pillow. *But she does not look like some beach shell.* Abby wanted to rub her back or get up in the bed with her, which she knew that she could not do, but that did nothing to keep her from wondering if MaDee was awake under all that sleep medicine and wanted her close. Abby decided to act as if MaDee was listening, and proceeded to tell her some of their favorite *Tiny Tamara Tales*. "Hey MaDee, remember when Mom was driving and she said that when she was on a long straight road that she felt like the world just had to be flat? Or, oh yeah...hey, MaDee, remember when mom would spell d-o-g, so that Rooney would not know what she said? MaDee, did we ever figure out why Mom had to s-p-e-l-l around the dog?"

The nurses were forcing large amounts of fluids into MaDee now, while Abby talked to her. Everyone in the room watched to see if the monitor would show some regulation in her blood pressure. Abby thought that MaDee certainly had to know what it was that they were putting into her now, because the liquids in the bags on the IV pole looked like icy slush and dripped condensation down their plastic covering. Soon, Abby knew, they would be draining them out of her again, almost as fast, and she hoped that once the fluid could escape, maybe MaDee would feel somewhat better.

All of these procedures had been done in the days before and Abby recognized each of them and all of the smells and sounds, but that did nothing to make *this time* any easier. She had started to become familiar with all the names and put them with the voices and faces of the nurses touching MaDee now. *Things like learning names comes easy*, but until all the fussing with her sister was done and the monitors and the drone of the machines had steadied, there was still fear rolling around in her gut, despite knowing the badges of those tending to her sister. “Hang in there Chrissy,” Abby said, using a nickname reserved exclusively for the two of them. “How about some more reading?” Because Abby hoped that the story would lull her sister back to sleep, she retrieved her book from inside her leather Coach purse.

Rhythmically, over and over, the ventilator sounded deep breaths for MaDee. No matter what anyone else was doing to her, this noise was the constant. The ins and outs of the breathing machine mixed with the beeping of the monitors. The red fluids being forced centrifugally to come out of her and into the humming dialysis machine were sounds that everyone expected now, like traffic around Dulles at rush hour. Every instrument that was in the room and hooked up to MaDee was mingled with the great fear of yet another strange machine that might come in and have to be understood. More and more metal machinery seemed to be waiting their turn in line out in the hallway, near the door. It was frightening to think that all of these boxes were keeping her sister alive; to *not* hear them through the course of a day would somehow now be strange and very wrong.

Abby knew that MaDee would be *steaming mad* at all the attention and everyone doing everything for her. MaDee breathed life into all who knew her and she could touch you, with just one word; yet the nurses had never even heard her speak. MaDee would not want anyone to see her like this now and Abby knew that if she could, she would sit right up and reach for the frothy latte on the table, beside the bed. Abby could smell its Starbucks scent and she wondered if MaDee could, too. It was MaDee's favorite brew and it seemed sad that only one of them could drink from it now, after all the times that they had shared a cup. Abby sipped the lukewarm coffee, set her cup down, leaned forward and placed the back of her elbows on the edge of the bed. She opened the book and began to read.

It was a little more from *In The Belly of the Beasts*, Chapter 12. *The Shack.* She read out loud, like an elementary school teacher calming and cooling her students, after lunch. Page 173. Jesus had been talking to Mack about Missy's last horrifying experience.

Jesus: "Why? Mack, there is far more going on here than you have the ability to perceive. Mack, she was never alone. I never left her; we never left her for one instant. I could no more abandon her, or you, than I could abandon myself."[1]

Reading passed the time and Abby knew that MaDee had planned to read this book. Listening to it now would keep her strong mind occupied. Glancing up before she continued, she looked at MaDee as she rubbed the crease between the pages in her lap. *I really think she can hear me, and, if she is half as scared as me, then I better read more and read louder to keep her mind off of things.*

Jesus: "She had no idea what was going to happen. She was actually more worried about you and the other kids, knowing that you couldn't find her. She prayed for you, for your peace."[2] Abby stopped reading to contemplate the words.

"We have to be strong," Abby said to her mom, who nodded her head three times in agreement. Tamara listened as Abby forgot her task for another moment and tried to humor MaDee into cognition. Chuckling, Abby teased MaDee, "...because if we aren't *stroooooong*, MaDee will send us home like she did when I went with her to school and cried because she was leaving me. Come on MaDee, lean closer to Chrissy. *Kissth, Kissth.*" Abby could always *steal some lovin'* if she came at MaDee that way, mimicking a toothless grin and smattering her sister's face with gummy, lip-smacking kisses. Tamara smiled as Abby pecked at MaDee, harmlessly. The brevity only lasted a few seconds, but it served to break the tension in the room.

---

1 William P. Young, The Shack (Newbury Park, CA: Windblown Media, 2007), 173.

2 Ibid.

MaDee hated it when Abby cried and she would be furious if Abby started now, even though there was no discernable command from MaDee in the bed. Abby swallowed the lump in her throat that came again from seeing no reply. She took one more sip of coffee, leaned backward into her chair again, raised the book back up right side, looked at MaDee once more, and began to read to her.

There were times when the bathroom-sized room in the Medical Intensive Care Unit was full. Tamara, Abby and the men who loved them, and the girl's dad, Tom, would filter in to sit. Dad, Abby and Mom had come up with a workable schedule for sitting with MaDee, over the last week. But, sometimes, the idea of staying with MaDee won over the one slated to be standing watch. No one wanted to leave her, any more than they could rest well when they did try to sleep. When the space became full in the room, it seemed everyone alternated between looking at MaDee and away again at the wall and then filing out, as only two could stay.

The things the doctors and nurses came in and did to MaDee were so intense at times that Tamara and the rest of them were only allowed to stand at her feet and touch her toes, while the doctors worked on the rest of the girl they loved. Sometimes, they instinctively took turns touching MaDee's toes. Often, they criss-crossed each other to stand at the bedside of her feet and hold the round, cold steel bed frame instead, in perfect but unplanned ways.

The men for the most part were quiet over MaDee, especially when the women were talking to her. But, sometimes, Tamara couldn't keep silent and she would lean over Abby's back, ignoring her daughter's recitation, gazing intently over her reading glasses at MaDee's face, just to make sure that she was still okay. If there was still nothing for Tamara to do, she would hum, over Abby's inflections and animated words. Everyone knew Mom was much too preoccupied to have to sit and listen to the story.

The car song. It was the girls favorite. Tamara thought of it now and she hoped MaDee still believed it was written *just for her.* "Abby, you know it by heart. We've sung it a thousand times before. Sing it with me now?"

Abby felt her mom's hand on her back and she heard her begin to sing. That made the lump form again. She would not finish this chapter and she could not sing this song. Rising, she set her book down beside the mound of MaDee's blanketed hip, turned and quietly left the room.

Jesus loves the little MaDees
All the little MaDees of the world
Red and yellow, black and white,
They are precious in his sight
Jesus loves the little MaDees of the world.

Tamara's mind swirled around the thoughts that formed in her head, like chocolate and vanilla soft serve ice cream. Tamara knew that she trusted in the Lord, completely, so she felt a bit like chiding herself for wishing: c*ouldn't this turn out differently?*

She dared to ask questions, but only in her mind and with her eyes closed and next to MaDee's. She was not yet ready to hear the answers from the doctors and if she leaned close enough to her sleeping baby girl, she did not have to think about them, either. *Could it really be that the plan for you is to go? Am I going to have to say good-bye? How is it that I can remember your first breath and how can I watch if you should take your last?*

"You are just a little girl," Tamara rubbed MaDee's forehead, round and round her brow, making circles with her thumb. Tamara felt the waves of tears behind her own eyes now and that deep dull headache that comes from a long day of too much thinking, too little food, and a very warm room. She leaned into MaDee and she left her mouth on her forehead, for what seemed like a very long time. These were the kinds of questions that had no real answers. *No one but God really knew how this would all turn out.* Tamara closed her eyes and prayed the kind of prayer that only bright and foreign hospital rooms, sitting beside a sick child, forced Moms to pray. Tamara meant this one, too.

Lord, if it be Your will, please don't take her away from me, again.

Chapter Three

The Ballad Of The Girl Who Wore Ribbons

MaDee Nicole Boxler was taken from her momma's arms, one other time. Born on the twenty-fourth day of October, in the year of our Lord, nineteen hundred and eighty-seven, she weighed in at eight pounds and fourteen ounces and she was every bit of twenty-one inches long, especially when she stretched. "She was whisked away from me," Tamara gestures wildly into the air, as if broad-stroke painting the words. "She was taken from us, mere minutes after she was born, like some button that you change on a radio."

"One minute she was there, and the next minute she was gone," she repeated again, for emphasis. "I really think that she spent the rest of her life searching for the love she missed those first eleven days." Tamara stated these things to no one in particular, as if it was all a matter of fact.

Her given name was MaDee. *MaDeé Nicole Boxler.* Mom had watched a show on television about a lady detective and her name was Madeline. Tamara liked the name and so she thought to shorten it, dress it up a bit and add a capital letter *D* and an accent mark over the *é,* if her baby was born a girl. Mom thought that when her girl MaDee grew up, she could be *that Dee.* The only thing was, MaDee never quite saw it that way.

MaDee came out yellow. MaDee was born looking as yellow as the sun a child draws on a wet finger-painted page. On that October morning when her momma birthed her, MaDee was as yellow as the sun's rays that poured into the hallway leading to the waiting room where her daddy paced. MaDee never minded that she came out yellow, but it scared her momma and her daddy, who could literally think of nothing else. Coming out as yellow as MaDee did made the doctors send her in a bed, far away, to get pink.

As she turned colors, in those eleven days without her momma by her side, the nurses called her *MaDee Nicole*. And when her daddy came each day to see her, he called her that, too. Her grandmother, the one everyone called Nannie, came to see her each night. She did not think she would call her MaDee Nicole. Nannie felt that there was just something extra special about this baby—something much more to this little girl—and she knew that she would have to come up with a name. So, while everyone waited for the baby's name to grow and for the infant in the clear bassinette to turn colors, everyone agreed who looked at her that MaDee Nicole Boxler sure was a pretty little yellow girl, with hardly any deep dark brown hair.

MaDee never thought twice, as she grew into a little girl, that she came out so very yellow. Being *yellow born* made all the stories about her growing up flavorful, like a mango juice and banana snack, dripping from a tangled up boy in a coconut tree. MaDee would listen over and over again to the stories of how she came out yellow. Her Nannie would tell them to her, as she ran ribbons through her hair, each day before school.

Nannie picked a name. She called her *MaDee Jane*. Nannie preferred calling her MaDee Jane, well, just because when she wore those white cowboy boots from Pigeon Forge to go see John Michael Montgomery, she looked like a MaDee Jane. Nannie liked the name Jane, too, from all the Readers in school. For little MaDee this was all just fine because seeing the *J for Jane,* sewn between the *M* and the *N* and the *B* on her *LL Bean Bag* was *so* pretty. Besides, Nannie said that she looked like a MaDee Jane. That was reason enough for MaDee to plan to add to her name, when she was old enough.

MaDee Jane. MaDee Jane Boxler. MaDee Jane Nicole Boxler. They all sounded good to the little sassy girl in the snow white boots with heels. But, if you counted Uncle Pete calling her *Wed*ge, because her bathing suit always rode up her *hiney* and her daddy calling her *Bomber* and then topped it off with *Sista Chrissy*—even though you *dared* not call her *that*—because that's what sisters say, well, you had a mouthful. Only Abby could tell you what name to call her, when.

When MaDee learned to spell her name, she dove right in. Spelling her name was like cleaning her room; there was just a way she had of going about the task and getting it done. MaDee's mouth made alphabet soup when she spelled her name for you and she even invented a few letters, too. When you asked MaDee her name, she would say, as-fast-as-she-could-say-it-and-all-in-one-big-gigantic-breath: *"I-am-MaDee-Capital-M-a-Capital-D-ee."* Now that *ee* she would shoot at you, on the end of her name, was the fastest gun in the west and a letter all of her very own creation.

A-B-C-D-E-*EE*-F....

MaDee would explain it *all* to you, v-e-r-y slowly, so that you understood. She would put her right hand on her little hip, cock her head a smidge over to the left, squish her little lips so that her right dimple showed and she would repeat everything, sounding a bit like a skinny high-pitched schoolmarm, with a dark and tall beehive bun: "I. Am. MaDee." Speeding up she would say, "That's Capital-M-a-Capital-D-ee, with a big *M* and a little *a* and a Capital *D*, *ee*, with an accent mark over the *e*, but you have to put it backwards on the second one, aaaaaaUND...." Breath. MaDee wasn't done. You had to hear about the heart. After she practiced that, fast as you ever heard, *ee* sound, she would spend days just watching her sister Abby draw those hearts. Lots and lots of hearts. Later, when MaDee spelled her name, or wrote it on a paper, or told you who she was, she had to tell you all about *the heart*. You see, MaDee had to make a heart right beside her name, too—just so you knew—she *really, really loved you*. Of course, this only happened after she took the idea from Abby when she turned seven and could draw a *good* shape on the paper beside her name.

Whenever anyone called out to Miss MaDee Jane Nicole Wedge Bomber Boxler, you could hear her sweet melodic voice answer you right back, and you could just *hand to the sky almost swear* you heard the sound of her smile in her cherry syrup twang. MaDee had that certain perfect smile—big and bright with very white teeth—a smile that would come at you, long before she did. People used to comment that they could hear that girl smile from a mile away. MaDee had the sort of smile that people watched. It turned up the bridge of her ski sloped nose and when she smiled her big wide grin, it caused both of her deep dark brown eyes to squint, like after the flash of a snapshot. MaDee Jane and her name and her heart and her big white boots and smile were definitely going to *boss you some kinda good* whenever she was around and answered your call.

Most of the family, when they think back on her now, can still hear the click-clack high-heeled wiggle of her walk. MaDee could come at you, *just so* that her boots would sound, even on grass. Her skirt came next. It would begin to swish-sash-swish-shay towards the sound of your voice and by the time she neared you, she had always just finished turning her underpants around and fixing her waistline. Everybody always wondered how she never hit a wall or a tree, looking down at that skirt askew and those boots on her feet. It was simple. She would explain to you that she hadn't *been just lookin' at them the whole entire time*; instead, she had *just begun lookin' at them.* MaDee would hear you tell her to watch where she was going. This admonition to look up would remind her to reach and fix those big colored ribbons on the top of her head, even though it looked like she was getting ready to dive into her boots. MaDee Jane wanted to look nice and it took awhile for her to do all this dressing up. MaDee Jane Nicole Wedge Bomber Boxler never ever minded the time it took to make herself look her best and all the ones who waited on the whole of her to arrive did not mind waiting for her, either.

Because MaDee was known for coming out yellow, and smiling all the time, with deep dark brown curls in her hair, and bright red cheeks dotted with that dimple, she thought it only fitting to have a *chocolate* baby, whose name, once she got her, was *Baby Mosey*. Mosey was as chocolate as a melted s'more on the front of a child's ruffled pink tutu and MaDee Jane loved her baby doll even more than she hated her very own hair. Mosey came with MaDee absolutely everywhere she went, except school, and Mosey heard *all* the stories of baby yellow MaDee, the things she learned in class and especially how good she was at *rummie-after-supper*. Mosey even knew that Nannie gave her coffee, too, and this was *something no one ever knew*, but Mosey was quite the avid listener and she could keep a very big secret.

Mosey and MaDee Jane wore ribbons in their hair, everyday. MaDee wore ribbons in her hair, quite simply because Nannie put them in there, but soon she grew to love them and put them in all by herself. Because MaDee hated her curly short hair, Nannie told her that "a ribbon can fix everything." MaDee used to wish to brush her curls *clean off her head*, but once she got those ribbons from Nannie in her hair, she stopped wanting to do that. Momma would drop MaDee and Abby off every morning to wait for school to start. Nannie would take one look at MaDee and her mangled hair and her pretty *I wanna wear this dress* with her white boots and she would go into her room to pick out a matching ribbon. Nannie told MaDee many times, "All the pretty girls wear ribbons in their hair," and she used to say, as she combed her granddaughter's locks, "MaDee Jane, just you wait. One day you are gonna be *so glad* you have curls in your hair...every girl yearns to have curls."

Nannie had so many colored ribbons. She kept them in a box on the top of the chest of drawers. When Nannie tied a ribbon in MaDee Jane's hair, you could smell the scent of vanilla on it, from the sachet inside the chest. And, when Nannie brought out a colored ribbon for MaDee Jane, she *always* picked one out for baby Mosey, too. Nannie put them in the girls' hair, just before she took them to school and by the end of the day, MaDee didn't see the need to take them out. MaDee and Mosey could play just fine inside Nannie's house with ribbons in their hair. MaDee didn't take to dirt so much. She preferred to play inside, where it was clean and tidy and where she could teach her dolls and her dogs to clean up their toys.

MaDee and Mosey went absolutely everywhere together. The only time Mosey didn't wear ribbons while going somewhere exciting with MaDee was when MaDee carried her by her deep and dark burnt brown sugar roots, which of course, made Mosey's ribbons fall to the ground. When MaDee Jane took Mosey somewhere, she loved to tell her stories all along the way…story…after…story…after story. The great thing about MaDee Jane's stories was that she always hoped that you would listen, too.

The ballad that you are about to read is one of Miss MaDee Jane's enchanting tales. It is all about the places that MaDee and Mosey went, certain of the things that they saw and more, a story all about the people that they really, really loved. This is the lore and legend of two little girls who just *hated* to sit still and who thought to wear ribbons in their hair, everyday.

Chapter Four

Spring Roars In

Spring is meant to roar in like a lion and leave like a lamb, but in looking back, the reverse was actually true. Early March was when things really began to blossom in Roanoke, Virginia. The trees were getting their leaves back; the flowers were budding and the grounds-keepers at Roanoke College began mowing the grass again, after the dormancy of winter.

In late March of 2008, I was in the middle of my second spring semester in college. I was determined to have enough credits to gain the freedom to live off campus, sooner rather than later. I even tempted fate by signing an early lease, to Salem Woods Apartments, banking on the fact that I would return the following autumn and move right in, to my very own place. It was a chance I took and it made me excited just thinking about it.

My friend Kacy and I had joined the same sorority, Chi Omega. We weren't hazed as much as we were stressed and challenged. It was a scary process for us, often bringing Kacy to tears. I never cried, from as early as I can remember, so Kacy looked to me for solace and we soon became very close, almost inseparable. When I love, I love a great deal and at first, Kacy was no exception. We were like sisters and having Kacy as my roommate made college feel more like home.

Springtime was busy for me. I was working for Big Brothers Big Sisters, volunteering my time, and my course load was strenuous. My Research Methods class was impossibly difficult and I spent hours preparing for this one single class. I would meet with my professor in the morning, attend his lectures in the afternoon and be back at work on his class in the library, later that night. I wanted to do well in my classes; no, I *needed* to do a good job in school.

Of course, I had time, as any college kid does, for sorority events and for keeping my closest friends, *the brat pack,* out of trouble. It was an almost certainty that I would be playing putt-putt and eating ice cream on a Friday night or attending one of the many parties on campus. On Saturdays and Sundays and over breaks, I would see my family. My sister, Abby, missed me the most, but I never allowed her to let on like that. Maybe I was mean, but I saw no reason for her to cry about missing me so much. Life was good, except for the pain.

Kacy knew about the pain. It would start in my stomach and literally paralyze me, until it subsided. I had to either lie down or sit very still when it hit. Because I was also nauseous and had a sore throat, I chalked my symptoms up to sinus drainage from seasonal allergies. But, I couldn't explain away that ache, deep inside my tummy.

My symptoms weren't constant, but they were consistent. This intermittent sort of scenario went on for a couple of weeks, often waking me in the middle of a sound sleep. The only reason I didn't scream out loud in the darkness of my dorm room was because there were too many people around and I didn't want to alarm anyone. Moreover, Kacy was a nervous sort and a bit of an anxiety-ridden girl; anything like this would have completely unnerved her.

I remember thinking that maybe I should take a pregnancy test. I didn't know if you got stomach pains when you were pregnant, but my limited knowledge about what was happening to me was beginning to cause me unnecessary anxiety at a time when my plate was already full of stress. I needed to find an answer for the pain. It came on so unexpectedly, and now, it was coming with more regularity and even greater intensity.

I reasoned that maybe I had an ulcer. I knew, after three pregnancy tests, that I was not pregnant. *The boyfriend* and I were on the outs and even if we were together, he would have run away at the sound of the word *baby*, so being *not pregnant* was a blessing, when I wasn't having the pain.

I called Nannie. She read me the symptoms of an ulcer over the telephone. I thought that all the hard classes I was taking and the amount of class work I had, plus the stress of sorority life might have added up and given me an ulcer. I wanted to convince myself that having one out of three symptoms of gastric distress was the diagnosis, but I couldn't move enough to think clearly, most of the time.

When an episode hit me out in the crowded downtown street on St. Patrick's Day, I squatted to the ground. The people above me were intent on the parade floats passing by and no one really paid me any mind. All I can remember seeing when I looked up was *green*, everywhere. I could not move myself into a standing position. I had to stay huddled down, like I was playing some sort of hide-and-seek game in the middle of the city, until the pangs—hot lava on the end of a red-hot fire poker—went away. Sometimes, they left me as fast as they came, but I never knew how long they would last; often hours, but at other times, only minutes.

When I was finally able to sit up on the street curb again, I had to have help. Kacy was with me that day and she finally got me to her car and away from the crowds and the booths that smelled like lemons mixed with campfire smoke. Kacy suggested to me that maybe we should go to the Emergency Room, but I was stubborn and I told her, "No."

I called Nannie when I got in the car. She told me to go to the campus doctor, on Monday. I also spoke with my parents on the ride home and they agreed that something was amiss and that I needed to get things checked out, but, since I had been having the pain for awhile now, that I could probably wait a couple more days to be seen. I agreed with them, but then the pain hit me again and that quickly did away with the best of my laid plans.

It was worse. It lasted longer. Kacy and I managed to eat an early dinner and then, as soon as we finished, she drove me to the local community hospital. When we got off of the interstate, we saw a sign for an urgent care, so we naturally took the turn into the complex. We thought we were where we were supposed to be, but we could not have been more mistaken.

The parking lot of the Urgent Care Center was disgusting, littered with wet and dirty bandages and old empty beer cans strewn by the gutters. There were many people sitting in their cars outside, in the dark, smoking and listening to music. I didn't see an ambulance or any signs for the ER Department, but I did see the lit up entrance to the Urgent Care, so we went inside.

Once we got through the rectangular glass foyer, the sights made my stomach lurch. The room looked almost as bad as a frat house after a big party and it had the smells and the broken and tired bodies scattered in the chairs to prove it. I instinctively felt like I was in the *wrong* place and about to enter a den of lions. This horrible feeling was confirmed when the attendant at the sign in station told me she didn't need my insurance card, only my name. I was further convinced that this was all a very big mistake when I heard the man behind me in line tell the same woman that he needed an *STD* test, but that he didn't have any insurance or a driver's license. She never batted an eyelid. He smelled of beer and perspiration. *What kind of place is this?*

I was in so much agony that I didn't think these things through or I would have left and figured out where else I could go. Kacy, who had come in with me, didn't know much more than me; she just knew that I had to do something. I had asked my parents not to make the trip to the Emergency Department, thinking I was there, but, once they heard about the look of the place and listened to the sound of fear in my voice, they pushed harder to come. I was trying to calm them down by telephone and keep them from making the trip to be with me. It wasn't that I didn't want them there; more, I felt like the sooner I could be seen, the sooner I could be released and if they drove down to be with me, it would be a huge waste of time. They knew about my symptoms and how bad I was feeling. Not knowing any better, we all agreed that I should stay right where I was and wait to be seen. They told me they would be standing by, waiting for news.

I agreed to call Mom and Dad back. *There's not going to be anything seriously wrong.* But, honestly, the more time that passed with the pain that would not stop, the less I believed my own story. The wait to be seen was about two hours, which I understood to be normal for emergency rooms, but that is quite a long time when you are hurting and have to go to the bathroom. This search for the Ladies Room became my first order of business, once I signed in. I found it and I walked inside, took one look at the sink and I turned to look for a cleaner place to vomit. The bathroom was worse than the parking lot had been, with stained wet toilet paper rolls on the floor and it had the smell of a week old camp latrine. I was so disgusted that before I even looked inside the stall, I covered my mouth with my hands, turned and walked out. I refused to go. I would rather have wet myself, first.

Finally, hours later, my name was called by a tired looking young nurse holding a clipboard and the door open for me. I was scared and I wanted Kacy to come back with me to see the doctor. The nurse saw my friend rise with me and before I could ask, she pointed to Kacy and said, "No." I asked her politely again as she led me down the hall, but she made no response. At one point I could not continue to follow her; I bent down and leaned my back against the wall, wiping the sweat from my forehead. I looked up at her from the floor and I asked her *again* if Kacy could *please* come back to sit with me.

I managed to walk the rest of the way in, alone, to see the doctor. I was directed to a brightly lit area with six beds, separated by dingy beige curtains, with what looked like shower rings at the top. I could hear the screams of a lady behind one of the curtains. I could hear another man, gasping for air. The stench was an awful mixture of urine, feces, antiseptic and latex. I felt like vomiting again and by this time, my legs were shaking so badly that I could not climb the step stool. Instead, I leaned, face forward, over the paper-covered table. The nurse helped me to stand up and when I did, I realized that I was going to be in a bed beside the putrid bathroom. I *told* the nurse, this time, that Kacy needed to be with me. She handed me a white paper gown, no bigger than a folded kite and a little Dixie-type cup which meant that she wanted me to pee in it, in the bathroom. She told me that the doctor would be in, when he could.

I put on the gown and I went into the bathroom. I was immediately overcome with the same odors and I squeezed my nose shut, hoping my dinner was not going to come up through it. When I saw my face in the mirror, I looked china plate white. I felt the need to run out of this horrific place and never look back and that is *exactly* what I would have done, if Kacy had not been there, sitting on my bed, waiting for me to come out.

Chapter Five

Puddle Wonderful

The ambulance ride to the other hospital took forever. I was frustrated. It was late and I was so tired that I couldn't keep my eyes open. I was lying on the portable stretcher all bundled up like a newborn baby and all I wanted to do was go home. At the same time, I was starting to panic. *What if they find something in my stomach...something like a baby?*

The ultrasound took place at Roanoke Memorial Hospital sometime after 10 pm that night. I had been forced to stay at the Urgent Care Center until it closed, waiting in that bed, in that scary place, for hours, listening to the sounds of sickness. The only thing good about the ambulance ride was that it was taking me out of there and I was told that I could avoid another emergency room wait by taking an ambulance to the *big hospital* across town. Because my stomach had not stopped hurting since the doctor had pushed on it, probing, I begrudgingly agreed to the plan.

I had bawled like a baby when the clinic doctor probed under my right ribcage. It hurt and I just knew that he felt something, because he kept going back to one area and pushing. He told me, "It is probably just your gallbladder." The doctor seemed to think that this was great news, even though he said to me, as he turned and left the room, "It will probably need to come out."

Doctor leaves; I cry. Ambulance comes; I cry more. The night progressed. Kacy was still with me, running interference on the phone. Uncle Charlie and Aunt Sara lived nearby and I called them to come, once the ultrasound test was scheduled. My sister and my parents wanted to head towards Roanoke to be with me too, but it was really late and they reluctantly agreed, after much convincing, to let my aunt and uncle handle things with me for a bit longer.

Sometimes, the blessings of having a large family and lots of friends comes in handy. I don't know what I would have done, without my family and Kacy there with me in those rooms sitting and waiting for hours for all the doctors to come in to see me. It was by now after midnight and I was having spasms. All I wanted to do was go home, crawl into my bed and forget this day had ever happened.

The ultrasound did not show *anything*; my gallbladder was fine. One of the Emergency Room doctors then suggested a CT scan. I did not want to have it done, but, in the back of my mind, I wanted to know what was wrong. My aunt had spent considerable time convincing me that because I was *already in the hospital* and in *so much pain*, I ought to have the second test. After some time thinking, I reluctantly agreed.

The next forty-five minutes were the longest in my life. I had to drink a contrast material that tasted worse than what must have been the spoiled, hot lemonade from the parade stands, mixed with the thick and dirty oil from the floats. I had to drink two large flimsy plastic cups of this mix before they would take me back for the test. Finally, in the wee hours of the night, I finished drinking and I was taken to be scanned. After it was over, about an hour later, they wheeled me back into the curtained area with the others and

I laid on the stretcher to await the results. Inside that curtained cubicle, after two o'clock in the morning, in the brightly lit Emergency Room of a hospital I had never seen or been in before, is where my real story begins.

Chapter Six

A Hard Rain's A Gonna Fall

A Hard Rain's A Gonna Fall

Oh, where have you been, my blue-eyed son?
Oh, where have you been, my darling young one?
I've stumbled on the side of twelve misty mountains
I've walked and I've crawled on six crooked highways
I've stepped in the middle of seven sad forests
I've been out in front of a dozen dead oceans
I've been ten thousand miles in the mouth of a graveyard
And it's a hard, and it's a hard, it's a hard, and it's a hard
And it's a hard rain's a-gonna fall

Oh, what did you see, my blue-eyed son?
Oh, what did you see, my darling young one?
I saw a newborn baby with wild wolves all around it
I saw a highway of diamonds with nobody on it
I saw a black branch with blood that kept drippin'
I saw a room full of men with their hammers a-bleedin'
I saw a white ladder all covered with water
I saw ten thousand talkers whose tongues were all broken
I saw guns and sharp swords in the hands of young children
And it's a hard, and it's a hard, it's a hard, it's a hard
And it's a hard rain's a-gonna fall

And what did you hear, my blue-eyed son?
And what did you hear, my darling young one?
I heard the sound of a thunder, it roared out a warnin'
Heard the roar of a wave that could drown the whole world
Heard one hundred drummers whose hands were a-blazin'
Heard ten thousand whisperin' and nobody listenin'
Heard one person starve, I heard many people laughin'
Heard the song of a poet who died in the gutter
Heard the sound of a clown who cried in the alley
And it's a hard, and it's a hard, it's a hard, it's a hard
And it's a hard rain's a-gonna fall

Oh, who did you meet, my blue-eyed son?
Who did you meet, my darling young one?
I met a young child beside a dead pony
I met a white man who walked a black dog
I met a young woman whose body was burning
I met a young girl, she gave me a rainbow
I met one man who was wounded in love
I met another man who was wounded with hatred
And it's a hard, it's a hard, it's a hard, it's a hard
It's a hard rain's a-gonna fall

Oh, what'll you do now, my blue-eyed son?
Oh, what'll you do now, my darling young one?
I'm a-goin' back out 'fore the rain starts a-fallin'
I'll walk to the depths of the deepest black forest
Where the people are many and their hands are all empty
Where the pellets of poison are flooding their waters
Where the home in the valley meets the damp dirty prison
Where the executioner's face is always well hidden
Where hunger is ugly, where souls are forgotten
Where black is the color, where none is the number
And I'll tell it and think it and speak it and breathe it
And reflect it from the mountain so all souls can see it
Then I'll stand on the ocean until I start sinkin'
But I'll know my song well before I start singin'
And it's a hard, it's a hard, it's a hard, it's a hard
It's a hard rain's a-gonna fall

Bob Dylan

I learned, early on in life, to pick my battles. I was seeing a guy that I knew would disappoint my parents. Living in the South, many supper table conversations are had over what other people *might think* of the things that we do and the people we associate with and my relationship with Chris was no exception. We had been secretly seeing each other off and on, but mostly on, for almost a year.

I wanted my boyfriend with me at the hospital. I really didn't care what my family or those alien *others* I had heard about, over dinners of creamed corn and barbecued ribs, were going to think of Chris coming to be with me. The situation was so intense for me there in that room that I needed him to find a ride and come to the hospital, just as soon as he could. After speaking with him, I told my family, "Chris is coming." I simply refused to talk about it any further. I had more important things to worry about.

I had just been told that I had *cancer*. The doctor delivered the news right there in the cold din of the bright lights in the emergency room cubicle. To his credit, the physician who was barely older than me, did ask, "Do you want to hear my diagnosis alone or with family?" But, his delivery was completely staid and totally *emotionless*. Although my world was spinning fast enough for the both of us, he might have done well to take a class in compassion and I might have done as well to warn him that I *never ever* wanted to hear news like that again, no matter who he was. I was devastated. *Old people get cancer. I was twenty years old.*

I needed someone to lay beside me and rub my back. I was tired, groggy, sore and very scared. I had cried more in one night than in a lifetime and all I wanted was for Chris to whisper soothing words to me. I needed to hear his voice and look into his eyes. I wanted him to calm my screaming head and help me to stop crying. Chris was, of course, completely devastated by the news. But, when he talked to me, he was more upset than sad, and he could only whisper, over and over, "Why you, MaDee? Why you?"

I did not have time to digest the news delivered to me the night before in the emergency room by the callous young doctor. All I can remember thinking is that Kacy and my aunt and uncle were with me. I was crying. Kacy was crying. My aunt remained calm but quiet and my uncle handled the news by asking questions. I needed to call my sister, Abby, and have her come, and I wanted my parents there with me, too.

I dialed the phone number for home, but I could not get the words to come out of my mouth when Mom answered. I handed the phone to the doctor and Mom handed the phone to Dad. It was explained that I was going to be admitted. The doctor mentioned tests and they talked about the next couple of days. I heard nothing except the word *cancer* and the sound of my tears and the roar of disbelief in my breath, and then, everything went black.

I woke up the next morning to the clank of the food cart, and the light pouring in from the hallway when an aide opened the door. I was in a room, with my family around me, on the oncology floor of Roanoke Memorial Hospital. I was told that I had been given something to help me to calm down and fall asleep the evening prior, down in the Emergency Department and it had knocked me completely out. I remember that my first words, when I opened my eyes, a few short hours later, there in that big uncomfortable bed was, "Please, someone, tell me that this is all just a bad dream." No one did.

A woman came into the room. She introduced herself as Dr. Melladi and she wore that white coat that doctors wear. She was working on a Sunday and she looked as if she had just showered and fixed her hair for church. She had on makeup and smelled clean and she carried a file. It was mine. She had some of the answers to the questions that we were all beginning to form.

Dr. Melladi showed us my scans. We looked at them on the framed light panel on the wall and I could see where this mass, *this cancer*, was located, but only when she pointed to it. It looked like some whitish cloudy whole grapefruit, with its contents spilling over; something very large and unappealing that I must have forgotten to split and chew. It was, the doctor explained, in a gentle tone, but with a firm air of authority, a mass located very close to my heart.

At this point, no one could tell me what kind of *thing* I had growing inside of me, but Dr. Melladi confirmed that it was indeed, cancer-*ous.* I was going to be scheduled for more CT scans and this time the doctor called them PETs. I also had to immediately be scheduled for a biopsy. Dr. Melladi asked the nurse when these things could be done and when she heard that it would be two days later, she refused to accept that kind of delay and she made things happen. The schedule opened up and I was overjoyed, because, in my mind, the sooner we found out that this was *all one very big fat mistake*, the better.

We all needed answers. A dose of hope. My family was reeling with the news. In order to know what kind of cancer I had and the stage of the disease, the doctors would need to insert a needle directly into the tumor. Dr. Melladi explained to me that she was going to go through my chest and take a slice of the tumor to be tested by the lab and then they would know how to help me.

No one with me knew what to do or what to think and we spent the day emotional, wrecked, tired, hungry and confused, especially my sister, Abby. If someone had looked down on the two of us, we might have looked like castaways, sitting on opposite sides of a palm tree, wet and hot, on some strange and deserted island. Abby and I alternated between feeling numb and wanting to cry. We all held in our questions and just tried to catch our collective breaths. We spoke about nothing of any significance. We looked out the window and we prayed, a lot. We wandered aimlessly in the hallways; alternated between sitting and dozing in the room. We bought food that no one finished and we took turns going to the bathroom. No one talked about the mass at all and everything we did say meant *nothing*. The big gray elephant was in the small hospital room with us, and there was no getting around him.

To make matters worse, two long days later, the results of the first biopsy came in and they were *inconclusive.* The biopsy they had done was considered unsuccessful and I was going to have to have another one. This time, the doctor told us that the best way to get the good sample that they needed from inside me, was to plan to go in under my right arm and through my chest.

The doctor explained that my tumor was growing rapidly and because the cells were multiplying so quickly, the new tissue didn't have anything to attach to in my chest. The facts were, that while it was still inside of me, much of what they were retrieving was dead. This statement did not escape me, but it confused me. Tumors feed off of live tissue. Was there not enough of me to go around? How could there be dead tissue inside me? I was still very much alive.

Finally, I grasped the concept that this dead tissue, from a live tumor, was what they had sent to the lab on the first biopsy. By now, we knew that they had to go in for more; that the tumor was occupying one-third of my chest and for the first time we heard that because it was *so big*, it was classified as a bulky tumor.

I was discharged from the hospital after the first procedure, with strict orders to return to the doctor's office at the Blue Ridge Cancer Center, in two days. At that second visit, the second biopsy was explained to me and my family in more detail. It would be an outpatient procedure and I would receive general anesthesia. This time the plan was to cut off all of the air supply to my right lung, deflate it, thereby reaching more active parts of the tumor, and, hopefully, obtain a viable sample. This was going to be done by using a special tube in my throat that split into two sections: one tube would breathe air into my left lung and the other tube would deflate my right lung.

I felt such discomfort after the second procedure. My throat hurt and because they had deflated my lung, I had a hard time catching my breath. It was explained to me that it would take a few days before I gained full air capacity, which was an understatement. I couldn't finish a full sentence, without pausing for breath. The doctor left orders for a breathing test a few days after I complained about my symptoms, which I found to be ironic, since they were the ones who had *shut off* my air supply in the first place. Nonetheless, I began breathing treatments, similar to the ones an asthma patient receives.

Not only had the wind been literally knocked out of me in surgery, so too had the direction of my days and nights been drastically thrown off course and I did not even have a good diagnosis yet. Looking back now, I can state unequivocally, that on March 15, 2008, my twenty-year-old life was flipped upside down and turned inside out, in ways that I had not thought possible. It was the beginning of an unimaginable year...in *hell.*

Chapter Seven

Love, Heart, MaDee

Chris was the love of my life, in an *off-again-on-again* sort of way. I laid eyes on him my senior year of high school. I was sitting in the bleachers at Fort Defiance High School, watching a cheerleading competition, when he walked through the doors and stood next to the basketball goal. I noticed him immediately. He was light-skinned, wearing Abercrombie, with a hint of urban, mulatto and muscle. He had a *big* grin that seemed to join the diamond studs in his ears. When his eyes and his smile met mine, we were like sun hitting steel over a deep Carolina blue sea.

Chris was a ladies' man and that didn't faze me one bit; he had met his match. I was a senior looking for a good time and he just happened to look my way. At first, we had a physical attraction with flowers and the excitement of intrepid and secret rendezvous. But, as time went on, Chris and I came to do all the things young lovers do freely, openly and definitely without much thought about tomorrow.

Chris had *attitude* and I loved that about him. We were partners and we danced in perfect unison. The music was always on—anything, from Amos Lee to R & B and Lil Wayne. We loved to shop, play basketball, laugh at the antics of Curious George and go on road trips. We quickly connected and our relationship grew, on a mental and physical level.

But Chris was a young boy—just a freshman—when we met. This did nothing to stop me from wanting to be with him and dreaming about the two of us, together. Chris was *definitely* front and center in my mind and I would have done anything for that boy, even in the off times, because for us, we were friends, first. Chris was a master at not acting his age and I fell completely for his swagger and garish ways, over and over and over again, like a child doing somersaults down a lush country hill. All it took was a call or a text from him, after a fight, and we would be well on our way to trying to work things out and pick up right where we left off. Both of us wanted to make a go of *us*.

Always living on the verge of a break up with Chris was exhilarating. I was a woman looking for love and finding it and I would put up with a lot; I tried to see the good in him, even when it wasn't always the best thing for me to do. I believed in second and third and fourth chances. Chris gave me all of that, and more.

Because we became serious and intimate very early into our relationship I made the decision to keep him in the cog of the wheel called cancer. Looking back now, maybe that was a bad idea, but I *really* wanted him by my side. So, when the doctor leaned the back of her hips against the medical counter, looked directly at me sitting on the exam table and delivered the news that I *might not be able to have children,* due to the toxicity of my upcoming treatments, and, further, when she told me, in that same conversation, that I should definitely prepare to lose my hair, I was completely and totally devastated. My first thoughts were of Chris. I needed him to hold me and buffer the shock of this overwhelming news.

Hearing that I had cancer was bad; finding out days later that I was going to lose my curly chocolate brown hair *and* that I might not be able to have children, crushed my heart. Every girl dreams of growing up, getting married and having babies. I wanted my fairy-tale ending, too. My world, the one that had reversed its orbit one short week ago, now imploded and fell to the ground, crumbling from the inside out, like a dove hitting a clean glass patio door. I was the helpless rock pigeon on the ground and all I could think of to do was lie there and wait for Chris to come find me.

Chapter Eight

How Does Your Garden Grow?

I had to act fast to save my dreams. Everything about me was about one day finishing college, landing a great job, marrying the love of my life and having a *flock of little ones* under my wing. My heart was breaking at the devastation all around me. *Wasn't it enough that I had to have cancer? Why did I have to lose my eggs and possibly my fertility too? And my hair? And my apartment? And miss my classes? And forfeit my independence? And my upcoming trip to Spain?* The list of losses was endless.

The emotional pain of sacrificing so much at such a young age was far greater than any of the physical pain that I was feeling. I was trying to secure a future with children, *my own flesh and blood.* I was missing so many classes and falling so far behind in school, through no fault of my own, that I had to run to catch up with *me.* I had at least one or two medical appointments every day. I was losing my independence at warp speed, spending more time with my family and far less time with my friends. I was losing my autonomy. I was losing the contract on the apartment and I was losing the lease on me. *I was failing.*

The doctors told me that living in the dorm or living alone in an apartment were now out of the question. Germs spread like wildfire in a world that was shared by others and worse, down the line, I was going to need someone with me, all the time. What *they* needed to realize was that I had to have time to *think.* I wanted to absorb the diagnosis and all the losses, by myself, but there wasn't a minute to spare for that, which did not sit well with me. I was sick, bitter, angry and I was, frankly, depressed. I lashed out at everyone.

I just could *not* make sense of why all of this was happening to me, especially during college. So, while I paddled through the muck with a broken oar, I loaded up a truck and moved into my Uncle Charlie's house.

I really did have a wonderful core support group, from the start. My friends and family had come to stand beside me, but all I wanted was for them to go away. I needed to shut the door on everyone and somehow find a way to absorb this set of events, before I could leave my life wide open. I have always been just that independent and cherished my boundaries and my world, just the way I had designed it. I wanted to keep things as normal as possible and being supported and catered to was far from everyday. The constant queries about whether I was cold, or thirsty or in need of anything, got old very quickly. I wanted nothing more than to somehow figure out a way to hold onto my world and keep everything the way it had always been. I was a *normal person.* I got my own water bottle. I knew how to cuddle under a blanket with a loved one when I was cold. I knew when I needed coffee. I had car keys and a car that would take me where I wanted to go. I was determined to keep trying to be *the old MaDee.* I simply did not want the pampering and coddling that comes with a diagnosis. Having someone always willing to take care of me and persons around me night and day was a constant reminder that, indeed, my life had dramatically changed. *Something was really wrong with me.*

My days of complete freedom were gone and the few choice hours of alone time I could wring out were dwindling down rapidly now, towards complete oblivion, like dirty drain water. I had a window of only nine days before chemo started and I had a future to secure, meaning that I had to act fast. Mom quickly made me an appointment with a fertility specialist that had to be sandwiched in between a bone marrow test and multiple appointments with my oncologist, who had suddenly become my new best friend.

A bone marrow test, or BMT, is the most painful thing I have ever experienced. Bone marrow testing was scheduled to determine the stage of the cancer and how far it had progressed. At this point, the chest biopsies had determined only that I *had* cancer, but we still didn't know how much of a fight I was going to have ahead of me.

The nurses told me that I would be numbed on my hip before the procedure started. I didn't think that I would need some type of tranquilizer or a sedative on top of that, but, I was *wrong*. Prepped for the procedure, placed on my left side, I was helped to curl up into a tight ball, by the nurses. As the doctor began to inject the needle, which was just about as large as a meat thermometer, she got only about a fourth of the way through my hip, when I screamed for her to stop. I needed something strong to help me tolerate the pain; I simply could not stand it. The staff was quick to oblige, and, thankfully, I don't remember anything after that, except that I was not able to put any pressure on the rear side of my right pelvic area for days.

I had Stage Two Hodgkin's lymphoma, depleted. Leave it to me to have Hodgkin's lymphoma; not only had I successfully done *that*, but, I had secured a top position in the rarest of the disease categories. This was not good news and I knew from my reading that this shot my chances of complete recovery into paper spit balls. Most patients in my age group with Hodgkin's lymphoma recover; in fact almost ninety percent of them do go on to lead full and complete lives. I had a subcategory known as *depleted* and I was the other ten percent.

The glass offices of the fertility specialist were gleaming, yet the faces in the chairs seemed hazy, locked in some sort of other-worldly time warp. The women all looked *deer in the headlight* nervous and most of them mindlessly flipped through two year old copies of *Working Mother* magazines while trying not to size up the females in the other chairs and wonder what could be wrong with them. The husbands all squirmed, picking at imaginary lint on their khaki pant legs or readjusting their heavy starch Brooks Brothers button down shirt sleeves, as if they would have preferred having a root canal without Novocain than to have been sitting in the woven cloth chairs that lined the blue and pink walls, wondering if they were the reason for another negative pregnancy test.

I remember that I had the appointment on a Wednesday because that day was my hard day at school and I had to skip another important class to make the trip. I carried my class books into the office with me, fully intending to read, but I could not concentrate. I was the youngest patient in the waiting room and when I was handed the History of the Patient form to fill out, I didn't even know what sort of answers to put on the questionnaire, especially my *reason* for seeing the doctor. I wanted to write in big black Sharpie letters, a message, like the homeless people on the sidewalks of New York pen on their tattered and worn cardboard signs. PLEASE HELP ME. I HAVE CANCER AND IT IS STEALING MY DREAMS. GOD BLESS YOU. Instead, I left the space on the page completely blank. I knew by now that no one reads those old and tattered boards or looks at the shattered dreams of the likes of me on a form in a fertility doctor's office. Thinking about all of this before my turn came to see the doctor, made me just as quiet as when I had a pen in my hand when the doctor spoke to me. My mom, thankfully, gave him the details, while I sat there, unable to believe what I was hearing them say about me.

I had just taken *three pregnancy tests,* fearing that I was going to have a baby. My mom did not tell the doctor this because she did not know about it. Now, I was listening to her practically beg for ways to help me make a baby happen. I just could not wrap my head around the change in the prayer. Mom tried to explain the parts that she understood, and as I sat there, listening to the pounding beat of my heart, the one with the tumor wrapped around it, I just wanted to cry.

According to the doctor, the process of extracting and freezing my eggs would take a month. I didn't have a month. The doctor took me off of birth control. He stated, as a matter of fact and with no discussion, that I "...would not be needing protection, anymore." My only options, in his opinion, to ever hope to have my own babies one day, was to fly to Ithaca, New York and have my ovarian tissue frozen by the doctors at Cornell University or immediately begin Lupron injections, at home. Mom and I knew, after listening to him and with little discussion between us, that my odds of a favorable trip north, given the doctor's report of less than impressive success rates with frozen specimens, coupled with my illness and future chemo schedule, made the thought of even planning such a trip, impossible.

I was going to have to artificially throw my twenty-year-old body into *menopause*. The Lupron injections would essentially cut off all blood circulation to my ovaries, which would thereby keep the chemo out of this sensitive area and hopefully preserve my chances of bearing children. This was not an ideal situation, by any means, but, if I wanted little ones to be a part of my future, which I most definitely *did*, then these injections, at seven hundred dollars each, over the next six months, had become a necessity.

The risk and gamble I was taking to do this to my young ovaries was tremendous, as was the cost, which was not covered by my insurance. But the risk of *not doing anything* meant more to me. I would not know if this stop gap measure had worked until I finished the injections and the chemo and waited to see if my menstrual periods would return, signifying ovarian function; then and only then, could I try to have babies. Until that time, I had done all that I could do, which felt empowering at a time when all manner of power and choice was slipping through my fingertips, like rigatoni water through a sieve. No one knew it at the time, but after I received the first hormone injection, I filled out the paperwork to adopt a child.

Chapter Nine

By The Dock Of The Bay

Before I could receive my chemotherapy treatments, I had to have a way to take the medicines, all of which would need to flow through my veins. Because my tumor was too big and too close to my heart to be operable, I had to think about getting a port, which is a name for a catheter that is surgically threaded into the veins that lead to the heart, with an apparatus, much like a soda pop top that rests under the first layer of skin. To receive chemo, once the port is inserted, the nurse pricks through the skin with a bore needle until she reaches the circular device, and secures the needle in it, connected to a tube. The whole process was revolting to me and I resisted getting the port.

I was taking the injections by this time, to protect my ovaries. The increase in my hormone levels did nothing to calm me down, emotionally or make me think reasonably or rationally. I was a menopausal basket case, on top of having mere remnants of my sanity left over from the news of the diagnosis. If all of that wasn't enough, my family was going through quite a rough patch as well when my treatments started. Things between my mom and my dad were not improving. Added to the mix, my sister was getting married and I felt like the drama queen about to fall apart on the church house steps. All of these events combined in me like gasoline and a lit book of matches and made for an interesting range and intensity of emotions at the start of my treatment. When the idea of a port was introduced to me, I picked *that battle* as one that I would win. I simply did not want it.

Poor Abby. I couldn't help but feel horrible for her. There she was, trying to plan her wedding with her *sick sister* taking up all the oxygen in the room. At a time that was supposed to be the happiest in her life, she was faced with sitting with her baby sister in an oncology ward, listening to her *growl*. It was she and Jeff, her fiancé, that did all the preparations and the planning for her special day; Mom and I were in no shape, physically or mentally, to help her.

My parents were trying to be strong, together, for me, but the truth of the matter was that their marriage was on shaky ground, at best. It was hard to be pillars of support, wobbling like they were. My parents wanted to be happy for my sister and they tried their best to be, but the two of them were, frankly, worried sick about me and stressed about the demise of their own hopes and dreams. I could feel the tension in the room grow whenever the four of us were together. We were all experiencing an enormous roller coaster of feelings, with great high plateaus and deep and treacherous valleys. My friends were emotional wrecks, too. They tried to hide it from me and they did the best they could, forced to enter a world that was as foreign to them as it was to me. No one fooled anyone. We had never been taught *how to be sick*.

The crazy thing was that while none of us wanted to remind me that I had cancer or ever show that they felt sorry for me, that is exactly what happened. I was treated like I was helpless and as if I needed everyone to take care of me. There were people coming together to see that Chris and I could meet; others were taking care of him, making sure that he was eating and giving him rides. There were people visiting me at the treatment center, from old friends to those *out of the woodwork, why are you here* friends, and of course, my family was by my side, constantly. There were endless texts and calls, more food than at a convention banquet hall and there was an endless supply of company. But, more than anything, I needed space. I needed time. I needed to go to school. I needed to flop down on my dorm room bed and sleep for days. I needed to go to a party and drink the night away. I needed to go to the gym. I needed to spend a weekend with Chris. More than anything, I needed the *time* to let this whole *cancer thing* seep into my brain. As much as my family and my friends all wanted to give me everything that I needed, there was no one who could give me space and time.

Chris tried the hardest of anyone. He tried to see me. He tried to call me. He texted me, endlessly. He tried to hold me when we were together. He tried more than anything to console me. He reassured me over and over again, at each visit, that he still cared for me and that he wanted to be by my side, all through the cancer. But, I became distrustful and I questioned everything he said and *all* that he did. He put up with my emotional tirades and outbursts, until he just couldn't stand it anymore and we would say our good-byes. Still, I always knew that he would come back.

I wanted to be grateful for everything that was being done for me and, seriously, I was thankful. I really tried my best not to voice my frustration at being *the sick one in the chair*, but it was next to impossible. Telling my professors that I was ill and asking for extensions and arrangements to make up my class work was not something I was proud of, or accustomed to doing. I missed classes now on a regular basis, not just for my treatments, but because after them, I did not have the stamina to attend.

Time in a cancer treatment center takes on a new dimension and it drains you, even if all you do is sit and get chemo or show up to keep a patient company. My first chemotherapy treatment was seven hours long. The drugs had to be administered very slowly to ensure that I would not have an allergic reaction.

I had won the argument against getting any type of port, especially the one threaded into my neck and leading up to my heart. My tumor was so big they could not put one directly near it. I was still fighting the idea of the pop bottle port under my chest skin. But, being stubborn meant suffering consequences. Labs had to be taken from my veins and chemo put directly into my veins by IV. I was adamant and I remained so for the first three treatments, but then, that too, had to change.

After labs were drawn on a chemo day, I would meet with the doctor and she would check me for any lumps, bumps, bruises or swelling and review my blood counts. I would get a physical and then, finally, the orders for my treatment would be written, all dependent on what the lab work had shown that I could tolerate in the form of chemotherapy. All of this took great expanses of time, but not the kind of time I was used to at school. There was no set schedule and the bell did not ring signifying that I could move on. This kind of clock ran on *hospital time,* and it was interminable. An appointment that began at nine in the morning usually lasted all day and the wait for each step in the process was grueling. None of the schedule was set up to include travel.

The treatment room was large, with twenty oversized brown leatherette recliner chairs for the patients, separated by a hospital type hanging cloth between each chair. Each curtained cubicle had a treatment chair, a bedside stand and a TV on a ceiling mounted bracket. There was no privacy; everybody watched everybody else get IVs, ports accessed, throw up, cry and talk with their loved ones. Some people slept through their treatments; others watched TV, usually much too loudly or talked with their visitors. No one could escape seeing the effects of cancer.

I was never alone; my mom never missed one single appointment and I literally had a crowd for my first treatment. But soon, the crowds dwindled. Abby came to as many treatments as she could take off from work to attend. A few of my friends were with me as well, when things geared up, but by the end of my treatments, there was just me, Mom, Abby or Nannie.

Everybody thinks that chemo makes you sick. It does. Fortunately, with the help of two powerful and very expensive anti-nausea drugs, I was only sick for two of my twelve treatments. Unfortunately, the first treatment I had was the worst in terms of stomach upset and because everyone was with me for that big start up day, I spent the day heaving and completely embarrassed to be vomiting in front of everyone. I think that was the pivotal day when

I began to think, *no one but my family should ever have to see me like this.* The nurses all reassured me that as my treatments progressed, I would be barfing one minute and eating the next. *Cancer is just that different.*

Chemo drugs are potent. I received a protocol with the sequence acronym ABVD. First, the nurses infused the Adriamycin, then the Bleomycin, followed by the Vinblastine and, finally the Dacarbazine. Talk about a cocktail!

The drugs literally burned my veins, hence the port I was refusing became an absolute necessity. Having an artificial means of delivering chemo right into the heart and not directly through sensitive veins was an idea that I still hated, but, the toxic medicines had caused my veins to collapse. I was forced to endure the surgery for the placement of the port, multiple infections in the line, stretched skin where they placed what felt like sharp glass underneath my first layer of skin, and an uncomfortable feeling in my chest, for months. The port caused me to be unable to wear a seatbelt when I was a passenger and I was completely frustrated to find that I couldn't sleep on my right side. When cancer comes, the definition of happiness changes right before your eyes and I just knew that one of the happiest days during this whole process was going to be when they removed my port at the conclusion of my treatment.

After receiving my ABVD therapy, I would spend the next few days feeling drained and resting at my uncle's house. In order to keep my blood counts, which are the marker of whether chemo can continue, from falling too low, I had to have Neulasta shots. These shots were designed to keep my red and white cells and my platelets high enough to allow treatment to continue on schedule. If my numbers fell too low, I would need transfusions and more importantly, my immune system would not be able to handle the chemo and treatments would have to be postponed. The Neulasta shots I received stimulated my bone marrow to produce the blood cells necessary to keep me on a tight schedule, but not without a price.

Bone marrow production feels like cement is being poured into your bones and over you while you huddle in the corner of a closed elevator. There is only so much space in the bones that house the marrow before the pain becomes intolerable as they try to stretch. It causes an achy feeling, like the flu, for days on end. I could not be touched, I hurt so bad. The shots cost seven thousand dollars each and none of them were covered by my insurance. I had to have twelve Neulasta shots. Even though I fought getting every single shot, refusing even one injection was not an option.

Chapter Ten

The Cancer Card

Friends and family will get you through some tough spots in life and, if they can't get you through them, then, usually, they will be there to catch you, when you fall. Advancements in research and drugs have made the physical process of getting the tough drugs—the chemo—somewhat easier, with the advent of anti-nausea drugs and pain medications. But there are just certain things no one should ever try to do alone. Chemotherapy is one of them.

Both my doctor and I wanted my prescribed cycles of chemo to be completed, but, each of us wanted this for different reasons. I absolutely *despised* chemo treatments. I wanted to live like nothing was wrong and sitting still for hours and hours, in one room, hooked up to a pole was like tethering me to a harness and walking me three times a day on a leash. It was *cruelty*. I fought the hardest for my own independence through my first couple of rounds of treatment because I wanted to believe that there could be a better way to beat this disease. I was *insistent* on trying to make the process of getting chemo more tolerable. I thought that doing this had something to do with having my own way.

Perhaps the idea of wanting to be this independent is foreign to many, especially family and friends who love you and who just want to help; stranger still, to the medical providers that have been *doing it like this for years*, but being by myself is what made me, *me*. The ability to go and do, alone sometimes, is *exactly* what I needed, at the time.

I never wanted to *pull the cancer card,* which is something that people tell you to do, when you want to be alone, or, don't feel like talking, walking or even showing up and it is used for the many times when you are too sick to handle the demands of normal everyday living. There was *nothing* about my character that made this appealing to me. I never made excuses for my behavior, my emotions or my whereabouts and it completely infuriated me if anyone thought that I should *take advantage of my illness*. What was even worse, by far, than me using this card, was when someone else tried to use it.

I learned a lot about people, right after being diagnosed, as I watched them navigate my crisis. It became apparent, very early on, that I couldn't let anyone stay close to me who tried to use my sickness to meet their own agenda. It was essential to me to be able to take a break from the cancer and all the mothering and the pampering, and when my needs were ignored, or my illness was used to the advantage of someone else, it raised a red flag for me. I guess you could say, I wanted to cater to myself, in my own way, despite and in spite of, the conditions and the people I found myself facing.

Starving off change and accomplishing any semblance of normalcy in my life meant that I had to honor and preserve two very important values—*truth and fairness*. When someone lies to me, I turn away in disgust. I detest dishonesty, in any form. Further, I cringe at people who derive personal gain at the expense of another. The idea that I was seeing people in my life who were now missing work to be with me, under the erroneous belief that I had to have them there or because of some feeling that they had that I couldn't do this alone, was the polar opposite of the truth, as I knew it.

The notion that because I had cancer someone should skip classes, or use me and my illness as an excuse not to attend to their obligations was preposterous. I could not understand or pretend to cover for anyone who said they were with me at my bedside, when, in fact they were not, in essence using my cancer for their own personal gain. I became completely wrapped up in the notion that this was not going to happen to me, and while the idea was a bit foreign to me, standing up for my rights felt good. I saw absolutely no reason for any of the people in my life to use my cancer, for anything. I would not be anyone's personal crutch and I did not believe that my friends should use my cancer as a cover for their own actions or use me to feed their personal gains and insecurities.

Because I felt so strongly about this, I began weeding out the good from the bad, in my relationships. I watched the way people handled my diagnosis and in doing so, this brought about the beginning of the end of certain connections in my life. Conversely, cancer was the impetus for new people to enter my life. God gives us just what we need, when we need it, but some things just take longer than others. Certain people will appear at just the right time, in the grand scheme of things, and not according to our own will. While the focus and the spotlight was on *me*, I wished for nothing more than to shut down the lights, close the heavy velvet curtains on the stage and keep all of this drama and attention far, far away. I did not want to pull my cancer card for anything. I did not even *want* the card, and, I certainly did not like it when anyone else used it.

But, come what may, there were snags in my plans. Cancer seemed to take the notion I had of handling things according to a separate agenda, however noble, and toss it to the winds. Soon, I had no choice but to start treatment, just like I had little say in the damage potentially being done to my fertility. I had no time to digest the idea of the port, once my veins were sabotaged. I had to take the hormone shots and the marrow shots and I had to miss many classes and more than a few parties. I had no voice in whether or not I saw Chris and I missed him. I felt left out of all of the fun my friends were having. I was tired, emotional and I was mad. I had to give in to the effects the treatments were having on me and on my family and in every aspect of my life. Allowing myself this one boundary, when it came to the use of my cancer card, was important for my sanity. It was my card and I was not about to use it.

I did, however, notice one significant change in how things were handled with me; first, I watched my parents accept my illness and, soon thereafter, accept, or rather, come to terms, with my relationship and my love for Chris. Mom told me, one lonely Sunday afternoon in the hospital, when we had talked about everything but the heavy stuff, that for her now, there were more important things in life to worry about than my choice of a boyfriend. While I was honestly gratified that I had the blessings of my parents in my relationship with Chris, it had come at too high of a cost. All I really ever wanted to worry about was who my boyfriend was and whether we would be seeing each other that night. The thought that cancer had played such a large and important part in convincing my mom and dad that I had made a good choice in a man did not gel with me.

I felt *terrible* about the chasms this illness was creating in my family. If I had forced myself to pull the cancer card, I would have wanted to use it to repair my parent's marriage. My mom and dad were living in a relationship that was over, for all intents and purposes, and it soon became my hope this cancer scare would bring them back together. I thought that if anything could be the balm and salve to their troubled relationship, my cancer would be it. Instead, my sickness had the opposite effect. My dad had started a new job and I was on his insurance policy. His job and the accompanying benefits became critical, once I got sick. Being the new man on the job, he told me, meant that he could not take a lot of time off to be with me, and as my treatments wore on, I missed him.

Mom took up the slack, like she always did, and, thank God, she stayed by my side. She was a long time employee of the school district and every chance she could, she used her accumulated sick and personal days to care for me and drive me to my treatments. We spent many a day sitting and talking in the ways that moms and daughters do. It's just that our time together now was in a cancer ward and not over lunch and a movie. I missed those happier times.

I was a *nasty girl* to my mom. Really, I targeted her; I was incorrigible. I could feel the meanness coming over me the night before my treatments, sitting in my uncle's house, watching TV. The stress would literally show up in the next commercial or walk in the front door, unannounced and simply overtake me. Just knowing that my treatments were the next day would cause such an inexpressible feeling of anxiety and an abrupt and noticeable change in my spirit. I think that because my mom was around me all the time and because she drove me to each appointment, I took all of my frustrations, stress and fear out on her. In some convoluted way, I equated her with the negative side of things, because she was always with me when the bad stuff happened and while this was no excuse for my actions and expressions, I think Mom understood. I know she certainly tried to. I had a million thoughts and emotions running through my head and at times it was difficult to control my hurtful behavior. I have always battled the *demon of quick-tongued retorts*. Sometimes, for me, it was just easier to lash out and think later—but it never felt any better, in the end, to do it that way.

I couldn't help that I was sick, but I sure tried. The only thing I had some vestige of control over was how I *reacted* to being sick. Naturally, I wanted to go and to do all the normal things; most of all, I wanted to help Abby plan her wedding, but my ideas were frequently thwarted. Still, I insisted on going places just to prove that I could go; never mind that I slept the whole way there, got sick once I was there and slept the whole way back home and landed in bed for the next two days to recover. Still, it was important for me to make the effort. I had to try to go and I had to try to do and I *sure as heck* had to make every effort to try to *be*.

I yearned for the emphasis to shift from feeling obligated to my friends and family for everything they were doing for me, back to the independent

MaDee everyone knew, who could control her life and take care of herself. It was never my intention to hurt anyone or make anyone feel unappreciated for all that they were doing for me, but at the same time, I had to pave my own way and that path was restricted in all of the important ways, which led to an overriding feeling of frustration. I bounced from one restriction to the next, like a puck on an air hockey table. Being so sick, I could no longer ignore sour feelings, misunderstood motives or petty grievances. Cancer was the great leveler and it was smashing me.

I fought back. I shaved my head. I did it for spite, after a *tiff* with Chris, but, mostly, I did it because I had that spirit of a winner, that competitive nature, that fire in my belly that comes from years on the basketball court with the guys, wanting us and them to win. I didn't cry when, early on, I took the scissors to my curls and cut them short to counter the bundles and strands of hair that were coming out in chunks and covering my pillow. But, there was something so unfemininc about taking a man's hair clippers to my head and shaving. It was much harder to do than I had imagined it would be. My dad shaved his head too, in solidarity with me, and while this was a gesture I took to heart, it did little to make me feel better, because I still had the mirror to face.

I was terribly worried about how Chris would react to my bald head, but he never flinched when he saw me and I was grateful that he was able to accept the outward physical change in me. I just wish that the two of us could have done the same with the disease *in me*, that we couldn't see. In June, just weeks shy of the end of my cancer treatment, I had to let Chris go. Chris + MaDee + cancer was not adding up. Now, right alongside my torn and tattered body and the curly hair on the floor beneath me, sat my broken heart.

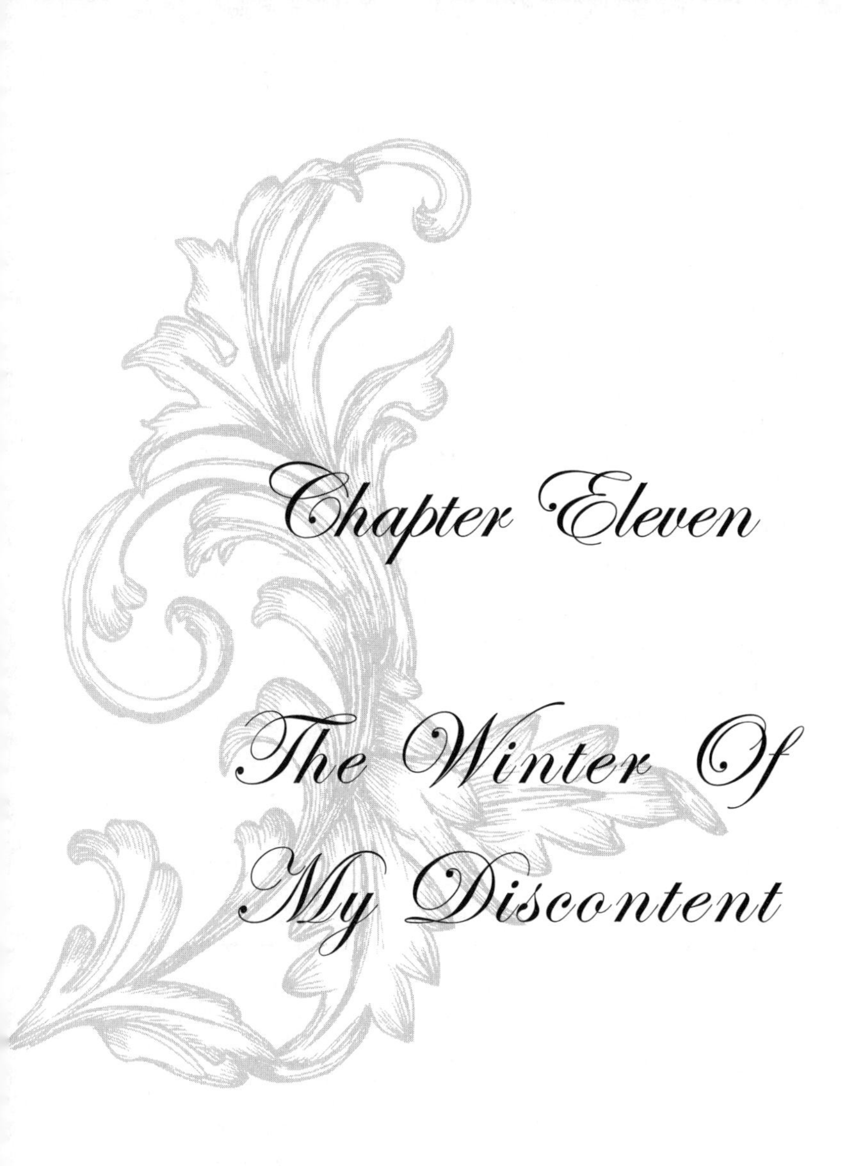

Chapter Eleven

The Winter Of My Discontent

Old man winter was about to come to Virginia, and, added to the demise of my relationship with Chris, my treatments were ending. It was a bittersweet time. I was finally going to be able to have the dreaded port removed from my chest and to celebrate, I picked a beautiful black satiny low cut spaghetti strap dress for the annual Spinster's Ball in December. But I would be going to the dance, without a date, other than my father, who would be my escort. The dance was still a month or so away and while I really didn't want to go, I did enjoy thinking about wearing that beautiful dress.

Speaking of beautiful dresses, Abby looked amazing in her wedding gown and we outfitted me in a Lynn Ellis creation that hid my battle scars. It wasn't that I minded having them, but Abby and I talked about it and we figured that *not having them* in the photographs for generations to come was a better idea. We both wanted the cancer to be a thing of the past.

I was simply *furious* that my treatments weren't going to be over before her special day and again, I let everyone, including Chrissy, know about it. I wanted to be *done* with my radiation treatments, so that I could walk down the isle of that church before her, leaving the treatments behind me like the sea foam froth of a summer's wave. But, after storming out and disappearing for a time, I thought about it and I calmed down. Life had to go on and I wasn't mad at Abby; I was mad at the treatments. When push came to shove, I had to admit that I was feeling good, and what better way to celebrate, than with a wedding. Planning Chrissy's bachelorette party and watching her become a bride were among the happiest of times.

I never looked back. Once I rang that *end of treatment bell*, there was catch up to play in every aspect of my life, especially my class work. The pressure was on, as exams were just around the corner. I was elated to pick up the pieces and parts of living that had been strewn by the roadsides of hospitals and doctor's offices and oncology treatment centers, over the last year. It felt *perfect* to have my old life back again. I got a special tattoo to celebrate and I treasured the gift box of baubles and new colored hair ribbons from my friend, Amanda. If anyone knew just a smidgen of the joy I was feeling at arriving at the end of my treatment, it was Amanda. After my hair started coming in again, I thought about her and her thoughtful gesture each time I fixed my hair.

I missed Chris, tremendously. I longed for him. We talked a few times during my first two months off of treatment and we attempted to sort through the remnants of our tattered romance, but I knew in my heart that I had changed and that our paths had diverged. There was no going back or making up for lost time and missed connections. Still, it hurt, losing him. My heart ached for him, right alongside that place in my chest that was bothering me, again.

The pain was back. I noticed that now though, it was more on the left side of my chest this time and there was a raised area that I could see when I looked at myself in the bathroom mirror. My mom and I talked about it and we decided that it was probably left over fluid from a pneumonia I had a few weeks earlier. We agreed I would get it checked out, after I returned from a tournament trip with the college basketball team. I was the scorekeeper for the guys, which was a job I had been doing for years. I was really looking forward to getting out of town and being with them. I wanted so badly to dismiss the pain in my chest, hoping that it was nothing, but *once a cancer patient, always a cancer patient,* and something inside my gut told me that I had better look at the scoreboard again, because I was about to fall terribly behind in the game.

I chalked up the exhaustion I was feeling on the trip out of town to the pace of the prior week of exams, the approaching busy holiday season and the bad cough I had battled a couple of weeks past. Before I could see myself clear to making an appointment with the doctor about this new pain, I developed a bad case of shingles, which is a painful, burning rash. I tried to fight it, but the pain was unbearable and I started feeling like I had the flu, which is another effect of having shingles, so I made an appointment to be seen. I remember that before I left for the doctor's office, I told my Mom that I thought the cancer had returned. It was just a feeling that I had.

I was right. *It* was back. I had essentially relapsed in just two months time, off of treatment. While we did not know yet the exact type of cancer that was brewing in me, my best hope, according to the doctor, was that it was the same type of cancer, returning. I had been told that I could get breast cancer from the radiation, but I thought that they meant much later in life. The chest x-rays, CT and PET scans all showed what looked like another tumor in my chest and this time, there was involvement in my lymph nodes under my left armpit. I lit up in the machines scanning me, like the holiday lights at a Pick Your Tree Lot. Here we go again. Merry Christmas to me.

I knew how this whole thing worked. Life essentially had to stop. Appointments had to be made, this time with a lymphoma specialist and a stem cell transplant specialist. A consensus was reached, rather quickly, among the doctors, that I had probably relapsed and while it was looking like it was the same Hodgkin's lymphoma again, a biopsy to confirm those presumptions had to be scheduled, and yet another port had to be placed. More chemo. Harder chemo, this time. I planned to do my treatments in Charlottesville, at the University of Virginia Cancer Center and Hospital. I would be followed by a talented man by the name of Dr. Douvas.

While dealing with cancer was nothing new to me—nothing that I had not been through before—that knowledge was of absolutely no consequence when viewed in light of a relapse. It was a bitter pill to swallow. In fact, knowing what was ahead probably made it harder for me to digest that I was sick, again. Cancer was beginning to teach me lessons that no curriculum in any college offered. I was now better equipped to handle medical news more analytically, instead of immediately dissolving into a quagmire of questions and uncertainty, but the constant state of worry, fear and the far-reaching range of emotions that had besieged me with the first diagnosis, returned with a vengeance the second time. My new medical awareness wasn't doing me a bit of good in the *deal with it* department. I felt the return of the loathsome beast that was totally controlling me and about which I had no control over.

But, then I would think about my family and watch their eyes mist at my news and I would listen to the doctor and his knowledgeable and calm responses to my questions and I would feel almost sympathetic with their plight. How hard it must have been for my family to have to hear the same news and feign stability; how hard it must have been for a caring physician to deliver bad news to unsuspecting patients, day after day after day. There is a sort of lack of control there, too. I can't imagine what it must have been like to have to always be so strong and steady for me, when all I wanted to do was crumble into a puddle of tears. This was probably the start of my class in *great lessons in humility*.

The winter weather in the Shenandoah Valley that year was uncooperative with my increased travel needs, now that I was being seen over the mountain and through the woods away. It snowed ferociously at times and covered the roads and interstates with ice and wreckage. It was a good thirty-minute drive over the Blue Ridge Parkway from my house to the doctor's office at the University of Virginia, on a good day, but on the day after Christmas, with the torrential snowfall, the weather made me late. Because I hated to be late, this set the tone for my first meeting to discuss the relapse with my new oncologist. Besides, I was starving, having not eaten in case I needed procedures that required fasting; I was furious at the traffic and the stormy winter clouds and frozen streets and upset that we were unfamiliar with the new hospital. Quite simply, I did not want to be *anywhere near* a cancer treatment center, especially the day after Christmas.

Subsequent to my visit, I was scheduled for the biopsy, and by virtue of being such an old hat at this game now, I stayed awake for the diagnostic procedure that Dr. Douvas had ordered. I had had so many procedures by now that I thought it would be interesting to watch one of them. I was sedated and I was numbed, of course, but I forced myself to stay awake, and watch the doctors insert the ultrasonically guided probe into my chest, searching for the abnormality growing inside of me. On the screen, it looked like a baking potato, long and oval and in a shape that looked entirely out of place, near my lungs and my heart.

Once the physicians located the mass, they made the decision as to where to obtain the samples and I laid very still and watched as they extracted several pieces of tissue from me, in the hopes one of them was viable and would afford me a diagnosis. They took six samples and everyone agreed that they probably had something to send to the lab. With that, the biopsy was over.

Round two involved getting another port. End of discussion. The idea was to take advantage of my sedation from the biopsy and my previous port site and reinsert it, thereby giving me two bangs, for my sedation buck. But there was an emergency that forced me to have to lie on the stretcher in a holding room and, story of my life, wait.

By the time they were ready for my second procedure, in a completely different operating room, my sedation had worn completely off and being re-sedated was not as effective. I was glaringly awake and not at all numb, like I had been before. The procedure was excruciatingly painful. I had so much scar tissue from the first port that putting it back in the same area was difficult. Had I known that it was going to be so painful, I would have asked for more anesthesia and gladly accepted the placement of the port elsewhere in my chest. The staff was accommodating and efficient, and thankfully, the procedure passed quickly. Menu for the evening following surgery: McDonald's.

The call from Dr. Douvas, my lymphoma specialist, came in early January, in the morning. The samples I had watched them extract from the recesses of my chest were...*drum roll, please...*inconclusive. Dr. Douvas told me that I would need further testing. Hearing this news, a carbon copy of the first time, set me up for the return of that previous feeling of frustration and anger, but now a new sense of abject injustice took over. *Out of the six samples they took from me, every single one of them were dead.* I was going to have to be rescheduled for a biopsy. My scans and my dead sample tissue reports were being sent to a thoracic surgeon, so that he could become familiar with my case and dig deeper.

I was going to have to be cut wide open. Dr. Kozower was the man picked to perform the procedure. His plan was to go through my chest, more toward my left nipple, and take a larger portion of the tumor. They could not take the whole tumor out because it was located too close to my aorta, again. Dr. Kozower planned to make two attempts to retrieve a viable sample, but he was very clear with me; if pathology reported back to him, while I was still asleep on the operating room table, that they did not have what they needed, then he would have no choice but to enter my body under my arm, in much more invasive ways. If that occurred, I would have to be admitted for recovery. I hated the thought of them having to cut me open like this, but, more, I detested the idea of an admission.

After spending an hour or so with Dr. Kozower, I was sent immediately downstairs to Pre-Surgical Admitting for testing, and, more waiting, staring at those black and white clocks on the wall and trying not to stare at the other patients in the room. I needed an EKG, blood work, a urine panel and I had to meet with the anesthesiologist. Finally, everything was all set for the next day. I was the first case, having been bumped up, on the OR schedule, which should have told me something. More snowy roads driving home with Mom, more McDonald's that night, very little sleep and we turned around and did it all again, the next day.

We knew where to park this time and the weather was somewhat more cooperative, and we were not late. Once I signed in, I was placed in a Pre-Op area, and after putting on my obligatory regulation blue surgical gown and those thick stockings that prevent blood clots, I was marked with yet another black pen, for surgery. Being marked-up so frequently in scans always made me think about getting permanent tattoos, and while the staff worked on me, I would make designs in my head of the ideas I could *ink* at the tattoo parlor. After I signed my life's fortune away with paperwork promises to pay, they weighed me, took my temperature and got the IV started, without too much difficulty. I listened to them tell me all of the *things that could go wrong*, and, I remember thinking to myself, *this is nothing that I haven't been through before*, which, in one sense, was a blessing, but, in my next thoughts, seemed to paint a very sad picture.

The very last thing I remember clearly, about this particular procedure, was being asked, while lying flat on my back, my arms outstretched to the sides of me, as if I was a female crucifix, "So, MaDee, what do you like to do for fun, when you are not in hospitals?" It was the masked and gloved anesthesiologist asking me this question, as he partially leaned against his black swivel stool behind me, in the brightly lit operating room, his hands just beginning to touch my face and neck. He was trying to be kind to me and he probably never really expected an answer. Frankly, by now, I was accustomed to the medical staff and their attempts to calm me down and divert my attention from the obvious sadness of the situation.

Before the friendly doctor administered the drugs that would paralyze my body and my thoughts, and, just before he reached for the breathing tube to put it down my throat, I decided that I had been quiet long enough. I wanted to answer him. I looked at him up across my forehead and I told him, “I like to do a lot of things.” I was just beginning to think about all the things that I loved to do and tell him some of them, when I felt the pressure of the paralytic medicines descend upon me. I saw the clear rubber mask and smelled the gases coming down over my face, and then, my world went black.

Soul mates, MaDee and Abby
Baby Mosey
Ribbons and Smiles

Mom and MaDee
My White Boots
The Middle School Gang

Nannie, MaDee & Pop
MaDee, Dad & Abby
CSI
ABERC ROMBIE
MaDee, Grandpap & Abby

That Smile
Those Feet!
MaDee and Mo

Chrissy

MaDee & Mom at "Wicked"

Baby Mosey

MaDee & Hayley

Grandma Baxter, Aunt, MaDee & Cousin

MaDee & Robin Roberts
Coach Mary
ROANOKE COLLEGE
Baby Nate

Cy
MADEE N. BOXLER
Mo

Chapter Twelve

The Damp And Dirty Dungeon

Just like a prisoner who marks his days and waits for little more than his daily meals, I spent six long days after the biopsy waiting on *the call* that would tell me what was percolating inside of me and what my treatment plan would be. I had heard words from the doctor at UVA, like *transplant, secondary cancer, progression, staging, muscle involvement* and, by now, I knew what these words meant. When I wasn't thinking, I was waiting and when I wasn't waiting, I was feeling mad. Furious was my reaction this time to the new set of symptoms and feelings this relapse was creating in me. I had always heard on the ward from the patients that *relapse was worse*; now I knew exactly what they meant.

I had leg involvement to go with the pain in my chest. It started as a numb-like sensation, in the back, down my right thigh. But then, it turned *ugly*. The pain was not prickly, but instead, it was sharp and intense, and it was difficult to handle, even with hospital grade pain medication, at incredible and increasingly frequent doses. I also had swollen and tender lymph nodes, under my left arm and around my groin. I felt sadness at the thought of losing my hair again and I found myself frantically searching the internet for shampoos, vitamins and follicle boosters, wishfully thinking that I could beat the medication's effects on my new short brown curls.

I had one week before treatments began and this time, I would be admitted for each and every round, which was not good news to me. I *hated* hospitals. They constrained and confined me and I felt like I didn't fit in, anywhere. Being an oncology patient in my twenties, I felt like I was stuck somewhere in between the children's pediatric floor and the geriatric floor. On the children's wing, with its brightly lit hallways, cheerfully painted walls and the Sesame Street uniforms the nurses wore, I felt the happiest, but it was rare to see anyone my age. The geriatric floor was just the opposite of pediatrics. Nothing moved, including the air, in the dark and dreary rooms of the old patients. I made every attempt to get a private room, so that I had at least the chance to make it mine. The residents, nurses and the aides did everything they could for me, willingly, but in the hospital I always felt like *a fish out of water*, on a cold, wet and foggy day, flopping in the sand and struggling to make it back to sea.

My first chemo admission went as well as it could. I was pumped full of anti-nausea meds, narcotics and fluids, before the chemo began. Since one of the drugs I was receiving was a steroid, I swelled up like a blowfish. My body was so puffy and my skin pulled so tight, that the whole of me hurt. The hospital grade chemo usually began on a Thursday night, when, at around nine, I would receive my first infusion. The next day, I would get fluids, which were given to flush the poisons they had just put into me, out of me, which made little sense to me. Then, more chemo on the second day. Some of the drugs took less than an hour to drip into my veins, but there were other medications that took a full twenty-four hours to infuse. Once I was finished with the first two days, I would be unhooked briefly and then prepared for yet another drug, followed by more fluids, until, three days later, I would be set free to return home. I knew the procedures by heart; I just wish I could have learned to sleep through them.

It was so hard to rest in the hospital and even harder still to actually get some shut-eye, during these admissions. The door to my room was opened constantly, with nurses, in hazmat gowns and gloves, bringing me the chemo, checking the rates on my pumps and readjusting them for air bubbles in my lines. Then, there were the inevitable vitals checks, sometimes once every fifteen minutes. Other visits were for administering stool softeners to counteract the constipation from the drugs, my anti-nausea meds to keep my stomach satisfied, delivery of meals, the plastic cups with pain medications in them and the visits from the doctors. In addition to the all of this attention, I was so full of fluids that I was urinating frequently, which involved shuffling with my IV pole into the tiny bathroom on at least an hourly basis, all through the night. Everything that came out of me had to be measured in a catch basin that looked like a white plastic hat with lines and numbers. I could literally watch the toxins and fluids pour out of me and into *my hat* at the rate of twenty-two ounces a pop.

Once I was discharged I would be driven to either Abby's house or Nannie's place. The trip home was always exhausting for me and I would fall into whatever bed I was sleeping in, once I got there. All I could do was sleep; I would sleep in very late, maybe get up to eat, nap on the couch, make it my goal to shower, and then go back to bed for the night. The first few days after chemo I always felt like I had been the mini car that Grave Digger ran over, to the delight of the crowds at a monster truck show. The fatigue that I felt after hospital stays was overwhelming.

Pushing myself, I would try to bathe. The thought of a nice long, hot shower once I was home was the dream that sustained me in the hospital. I would look forward to it all weekend. I can remember once, at Abby's house, stepping into the warm water, rinsing myself and beginning to put the coconut smelling shampoo into my hair, when, all of a sudden, the chemo caught up to me. I doubled over, squatted down and closed my eyes to stop the spinning, letting the soapy water cascade unchecked, into my ears and over my back, like an overturned kayak after the crest of the falls. All I could do was cry at the total humiliation I felt needing help with something as simple as a shower. The complete loss of any semblance of control or privacy there in that bathroom tub practically shattered my spirit.

Abby and Mom were always nearby, waiting and listening for me to wake up, to need anything or to want something to eat. Abby and I had a routine. She would sit in bed with me for hours, watching TV or talking with me. When I got tired, she would rub me down with lotion. Chemo had made me unable to tolerate perfume or any strong smells, so we took to using Johnson's Lavender Baby Lotion and I would smell it as I drifted off to sleep. Abby would then slip my college blanket over me and then, I would feel her slip away, only to see her smiling face return to the door when she heard me wake up.

Abby seemed to know what I wanted to eat and when, instinctively, and she ate it all with me, in an effort to keep me nourished. She would lay beside me, telling me stories of her day, the crumbs and crackers just whisked off of the bed with no consequence, falling like snowflakes on the floor. How I loved listening to Abby's stories and laughing with her.

I can remember one particular evening when Abby finally *gave in* to my constant and steady nagging and pleas for a shower, and even though she chided me for trying to do it alone, she left me in the bathroom, by myself. I kept the door cracked and I knew she was close by, but I coveted the privacy of undressing and washing myself; but, it wasn't three minutes later when I had to scream for her. I was dizzy and again I could not stand up and the whole *I'm naked and I can't even bathe* humiliating feeling made me start to cry. But Abby had this way about her of calming me. She ignored my pitiful stance and my tears, too. She would gently open the curtain, step into the tub, completely clothed, and, leaning over me, she would finish washing my head and lathering my back. I could feel her arms touching me as I cowered, weakly, in the water. Usually, after she was done with my back, I would have recovered enough strength to stand up and finish washing myself, but it took all of my energy and every ounce of my strength to complete such an ordinary task. The idea that I depleted my entire tank of resources with the single and simple act of washing, was just another thing to add to the many things that had been taken from me; a list that I had always taken for granted.

It's not the cancer that kills you, usually. People talk during treatments, sitting in the chairs, and I had always heard this. It is the side effects of the drugs given to you to save your life that will *nail* you and such was the case with me. I was back on the Neulasta shots. They were given to me to keep my immune system strong and to prevent my blood counts from falling dangerously low, where any sort of bacteria in our everyday world could cause severe and sometimes fatal infections in an immune compromised host, namely, me. So, when the toilet bowl turned red, I knew that I had more going on than could be attributed to the side effects of chemo.

One more drug was added to my arsenal of medications, making my family feel like pharmacists with so much medicine to give me every day. Having them stand over me with yet another pill to take made me feel more like a five-year-old child, forced to eat her peas before dessert. I could not bathe, live on my own or be left alone for an instant, even though I really believed that I could *look both ways all by myself* before I crossed the street. Needless to say, I slept through the majority of these childish emotions and the pain, too.

I hate medicine, I really do. I hate labels as well, like *cancer patient*, or, *needy* and especially, *depressed.* I was trying to hold back a flood of these tags, in addition to the new sign I got to hold, signifying relapse. I was worried and I was completely and totally exhausted. I was saddened to my core at the inability of my parents to patch up their marriage. I fought tears, constantly. As I sat in the waiting room of the doctor's office, for perhaps the one-hundredth time, I remember noticing that familiar and nauseating *déjà vu* come over me. It made me squirm, moving uncomfortably in my chair, as if to get away from myself. *Haven't I already done all this? Wasn't once, enough?*

I did not want the old feelings of *chemo brain* to come back. Chemo brain feels like a hot sticky web of confusion, as if walking through the forest at night, with no flashlight. I had no patience anymore—not for petty and certainly not for drama—and I was tired of feeling *weird* all the time. I knew that I was depressed and I thought that I would probably ask for antidepressants. But the notion of adding another drug alarmed me. In addition, I would also have to begin to house the notion that I had again *failed to handle it all* and that I was not *woman enough* to manage things. I had always been my own source of strength; I had always been the *helper*, and now I was the one needing the help. *If I start taking antidepressants, isn't that admitting the cancer is getting the best out of me?*

I caved, practically the moment the doctor walked into the examination room. He cheerfully said hello and asked me how I was doing and instantly, my tears told him everything. Oncologists have a remarkable ability to almost *see* cancer, before they read the labs, and their assessment of the patient often takes into account a great deal about what they observe, when they come in to the room. I had heard the words, "You are really looking *great*, MaDee," so many times before and I knew that it implied that, perhaps, they were expecting me to look worse. Now, I was *worse*.

When I sat and cried in response to the doctor's greeting, I am sure that he knew that all was not sitting right in my world. Dr. Douvas and I talked about the harsh chemo I was receiving and the emotional side effects it was likely having on me this time around. I had never even considered the notion that half of what I had been feeling was *directly attributable to the chemo.* I had always blamed myself for all of my moods and my seeming inability to get and keep a grip. The doctor was comforting and he really seemed to empathize with what I was feeling, almost as if he had felt the same things, too. He told me of a young lady, like me, that he had once treated. This former patient of his had a medical situation similar to mine and she had beaten the odds and come out of the treatments successfully and what's more, she was still doing well. Dr. Douvas gave me hope that day and a prescription for antidepressants. I filled the script, got a ride to Nannie's house and slept, for two days straight. I felt more like myself and jumped right back into the ring, when I finally woke up.

I was learning, faster, this time. I was asking for more help and I was beginning to accept the help that was offered. I really tried to be more gracious to my mom and to my family, the second time around, despite the increased intensity of the treatment and the horrible moods I was experiencing. I was becoming a seasoned pro at this thing they called cancer and while it still made me madder than a hornet to even have to be dealing with this disease,

I had the inkling that I was in the early stages of also swallowing heaping spoonfuls of attitude and gratitude, which are two more subjects they didn't teach me in school.

When I slipped, when I faltered, when I became angry and lashed out at those standing helplessly and hopefully beside me, it was the cancer speaking; not me. I was coming to grips with the idea that in order to fight the beast, I could not struggle against it and especially not against the people who were trying to help me. I was beginning to swim with the current and not upstream, without a paddle. I was learning to accept the tides. Even though I felt like I was being treated like a child and that no one was listening to me, looking back, I see that I was beginning to come to the realization that I had been taken prisoner, far before the cancer diagnosis. I was a young woman held hostage to old ways and outmoded beliefs that had no real substance or use for me now. No one and *no thing* was going to make my excuses, moods, wishes or dreams viable now, unless I changed the one area that I *could* control: my attitude. I was destined to receive, without ever having asked, some of life's most important lessons and it was going to be up to me whether or not I outstretched my hand and accepted them, or blindly kept throwing punches into the air.

Chapter Thirteen

Then Came Theogeny

If I was going to spend all of my life air punching cancer dragons in the dungeons, the least I could do was look good while doing it. I have always loved jewelry. One of my favorite gifts to give and to receive has always been little velvet boxes, with shining trinkets inside. So, when *Pandora* launched its signature charm bracelet, with portions of every charm sale going to support the Susan G. Komen Breast Cancer Foundation, I began wanting more than one. I loved the individual nature and symbolism of every glass bead available to put on their ropes. I admired the ads about their jewelry and how it had the magical ability to *color my world.* I could identify with *Pandora's* slogan, wanting me to tie *the perfect knot*, in the very short string I was hanging onto, for dear life. I knew all the recent company designs, and I really wanted a bracelet so that I could begin collecting the charms.

Every piece of clothing that I owned had at least one bedazzling *bling bling* to go with it, even my sweats. I could think of quite a few beautiful charms made by Pandora that would not only look fantastic on my wrist but would represent my life's journey and all the things that I loved doing. But, what I did not know, was that Pandora had a box.

Pandora comes to us from Hesiod's epic poem, *Theogeny* and his subsequent piece, *Works And Days*. In the first narrative we learn of the origin of a woman and moreover, all about the scope of her misery in a world fraught with confusion and chaos.[1] *Gosh this is starting to sound familiar.* This woman in the poem is created by Hephaestus, a

1 Hesiod, *Theogeny*, lines 507-510, tr. Hugh G. Evelyn-White [1914].

Greek God, similar to Vulcan, the mythological god of fire, but as the epics progress, more gods contribute to her being. Athena, for instance, teaches her weaving and needlework; Aphrodite *shed grace upon her head and cruel longing and cares that weary the limbs.* Hermes gave her a mind and also the power of speech. Athena then clothes this beautiful woman, and finally, the goddesses, Persuasion and Charities, adorn her with a garland crown, necklaces and other jeweled finery.[2] *Ok, I get it. The jewels.*

Hermes gives this woman a name. She is called Pandora, which means, *all-gifted,* as in, each Olympian gave her a gift. She then appears before her people with a jar or, in most stories, a box, containing *burdensome toil and sickness that brings death to men, diseases and a myriad of other pains.* Epimetheus accepts this new goddess, Pandora, despite being warned about her box. Immediately, Pandora scatters the contents of her box around the gods and, as a result, Hesiod tells us, sadly, *the earth and sea are full of (her) evils.*[3]

Now this set of despicable circumstances might have been cause extraordinaire for me not to have ever even considered wanting to purchase a band, had I known about the evils, *but for,* the ending of this tragic myth. One very particular item did not escape the box, in the story of Pandora. The one single, solitary thing left in the unbreakable box was hope. *Hope was the only thing that remained under the lip of the jar and did not fly away.*[4]

---

2 Hesiod, *Works And Days*, lines 60-68, tr. Hugh G. Evelyn-White [1914].

3 Ibid. lines 90-105.

4 Ibid. lines 96-99.

Funny, how hope was really all I had left in my box of tricks, too. I never really understood why hope remained in Pandora's box, but I am sure glad that it did.

I had a plan for transplant in place, rather early on into this relapse. And, now I also had additional doctors on my team of providers. It was agreed by all concerned that before I could harvest my cells, they needed to be mobilized, and before they could be mobilized, they had to be collected and before they could be collected, they had to be cancer free—no small task—given my track record.

I would have to be admitted for additional rounds of chemo before any more talk of transplant was going to occur, because the ideal situation would be for all of the cancer cells in me to be gone, before transplant. This made no sense to me and I wrestled with the conundrum and the logic of this requirement. *Why do I need a transplant if all the cells after chemo were cancer free without it? If the cancer is gone in the first place, then why do the transplant?*

It was a frustrating time for me, not only because I really did not understand the reasoning of the doctors, but more, because the time frame whereby they were looking at sending me to transplant was going to be my last free summer before I graduated from college. It was the time when I had planned to find a job, make plans for the future, have my last flings, *sew my wild oats*. I just could not wrap my head around the fact that I would be spending that last bit of free time in a student's world, in transplant.

Nothing seemed to go as planned during the next month of treatments, further contributing to the overriding feeling that the calendar of events leading to the optimum transplant time, was not looking good. I was rescheduled continuously and I grew increasingly frustrated with hospitals, admissions, policies and procedures. Looking back, it was no wonder I was fraught with delays. The law of averages eventually catches up with you, once you have been a cancer patient long enough. After roughly one hundred admissions and visits, statistically speaking, my number had come up.

Chemo treatments were still, thankfully, pretty much the same. They were starting to feel like clockwork and actually more normal to receive than to not receive, as convoluted as that notion was for me. I was being treated aggressively, but *softly*, somehow; in other words, the treatment was tolerable. I would receive literally liters of IV fluids, try to sleep through twenty-four hour infusions, and constant interruptions and I still detested the hospital food, but nothing was terribly amiss. I considered these days, *easy* days, which was yet another ironic twist in my life's view of things and, not that I knew it then, but was going to prove to be the understatement of my life.

The chemo this time did do more damage to my stomach and the nausea was relentless. I lived with a horrible metallic taste in my mouth, which made almost all food unpalatable. It was such a treat when Nannie would bring me a home cooked meal. Her food was the only thing I could eat; everything else I tried to ingest tasted like the inside of a bag of computer chips.

During my treatments, I was constantly hooked up to chemo on the IV pole and I was unable to leave my room, so I especially enjoyed the visits from family, friends, and especially the ones from people bearing babies for me to cuddle and kiss. I also loved talking with the precious *little ones* getting treatments and staying in the rooms beside me. It was love at first sight for me and these children. They had a great deal to teach me, especially when it came to making those nurses do their jobs. I learned more about IV poles and beeping machines from a five-year-old named Hayley, than I ever could have been taught in medical school, and there was nothing sweeter than a hug and a snuggle in the hospital bed from her. Our families enjoyed the camaraderie and the exchange of hugs, morale boosters and stories; simply the kind of understanding that only those in the trenches of treatment could know about, without even saying a word.

I loved discharge day. Getting my walking papers and feeling the sun shine on my face once I was discharged, was wonderful. But, I still couldn't be alone after treatments, so I immediately began to feel like I was that child forced to the babysitter's when I walked out of the hospital doors. I wanted to taste food again; I needed to feel the fresh air on my face and, more than anything, I longed to be free.

Abby knew, sometimes before I did, just what I most desired. She knew that I had to get a little down time by myself. Sometimes, it is the little things that make the most difference during cancer, and, for me, it was a morning, alone. I desperately needed to think and I could not do that in the hospital or at home, under the watchful eyes of my family. I did not even listen to music when I stayed with others and it was difficult to always be the guest, even among family. Abby knew this and she acquiesced. Once. She left me alone for one brief morning, while she went to church. During that time, I fell, in the shower. When she returned, she felt such guilt for ever having left me that her sadness, in turn, made me feel horrible for ever having asked. And, frankly, crawling out of the shower, naked, half-cleaned, half-soaped and terrifyingly weak, dizzy and much too tired to dress or to do more than lie catatonic on the bed, under the spread, was becoming a habit. After my morning alone, I gave up. I did the only fair thing. I quit asking.

Chapter Fourteen

The Mustard Seed

God plants people and certain ideas into our hearts and in our minds, when we are ready. I thought I had reached that point and I called my doctor and I told him so. I wanted more than anything to move up the date of my transplant, by two months; March, instead of May. I thought that I had come up with a great plan. I wanted to stop my treatments; hook the ball to the left, and throw a strike.

But, according to the doctor, there were hurdles. I had to have insurance company approval. Check. I had to have the agreement of the doctors who were looking to treat me during the transplant. By telephone and through emails, they agreed. Done. Finally, I was told that I would have to have a clean PET and CT scan at UVA. This would be the first scan since my relapse in December and *scanxiety* quickly set in, along with the interminable delays, frustrations and nuisances of my particular case, all of which I was trying so hard to control.

On March 11, 2009, I had the scan. It was a gloomy, snowy day and I was again agitated at being late, more aggravated at having to wait and almost ready to draw my own labs after being stuck five times in collapsed veins. Finally, I was taken back to Nuclear Medicine and injected with a radioactive tracer, which sat in my organs for over an hour and a half.

The scan itself took only thirty-five minutes, followed by ten minutes on the table waiting to see if the pictures had turned out. I was ravenous by this late hour in the afternoon, having not eaten since nine o'clock the night before. Two things that get my goat: being hungry and having to wait. Now I waited, starving.

I should warn you. *Never* get a scan result on Friday the thirteenth. I was determined to have my transplant moved up, just as Dr. Douvas and I had talked about the week prior. When he opened the door to my exam room with the results in his hands, I could see him smiling. My plan gained momentum as soon as he said to me, "You can relax! It's good news!"

But, it wasn't good news to me. As he explained the findings of the CT scan, all I could feel was the shattering of my hopes, one more time. I was going to have to have two more treatments, over the next seven weeks. Never mind that the ICE chemo regiment was working well; all I heard him say was, "More chemo, MaDee."

I really did receive excellent news about the progression of the tumor and my lymph node involvement, but, the listener has to be ready. I was not. I also heard him say something about *tracer in my marrow* and I added this new finding to the ladder of disappointments that reached far down into the dungeon. I had seven more weeks to go, before I could even remotely think about getting to transplant. *What if it comes back in the meantime*? I was staring down a twenty-five to fifty percent chance of rapid recurrence.

As I was fighting back the tears, the nurse accessed my port and began giving me a bolus of fluids. I literally went straight from Dr. Douvas' office to the hospital, where I was admitted for round three. I spent the night alone in a private room, with my thoughts. I was really thankful that no one stayed with me that evening, because my mood was horrendous. Once again, the thing that I needed everyone to do, in the face of this news, was to leave me alone to come to terms with this latest setback. Finally, I had the one thing that I had been screaming for—I was alone—and I had time to think. Funny how things work. For the first time, I did not like it.

I watched a movie that night. It was called, *The Bucket List*. In the film, Jack Nicholson and Morgan Freeman go on a road trip with a wish list of things they want to do before they die...before they *kick the bucket*. Both men are terminally ill and I was beginning to think that I might be, too. I made a bucket list that same night, in the off chance that God had different plans for me. It was the first time and the only time that I wrapped my arms around myself in the dark hospital room bed and cried myself to sleep.

The next day, my room was bustling with cheerful nurses, aides taking my vitals, techs getting blood from me and the RNs starting the infusions. I had a room full of visitors which took my mind off of my heartache. I can remember laughing to myself at the irony of my situation. Here I was, sitting in a bed in an out of town oncology ward, relapsed, with marrow involvement, watching *old men movies* about preparing to die. Fast forward, and in the next scene, I am talking to my best friend, Amanda, whose mother had fought breast cancer, about *my* cancer. Here she was, spending all day with me, away from her own family and friends and we are whispering together like on an overnight sleepover about the worst of our fears, the horror of treatment and each and every one of my complaints. I could *really* talk to Amanda—*she got it*. But the irony that was not lost on me is that we were two *twenty-somethings, exchanging notes on cancer.* Leave it to Amanda, though; she had me laughing in the bed, beat bopping and rapping to the sounds of Lil Wayne on the radio, in record time. She was an amazing woman. Nothing made much sense anymore and Amanda made that all seem okay.

I decided after spending the night with her, that I would rally the troops. I opened a CaringBridge page. This was a way I could communicate with all of my friends and family, in journal fashion. I knew, from hanging around with Amanda the day before, that I was sorely missing my friends and I realized that they were going to be just the medicine I needed, to soothe my damaged soul. Even though the anger came and went inside me at being diagnosed for a second time, I knew I needed to connect with the outside world in order to stay positive. Finally, I was coming out of my shell.

I remember looking back at my first CaringBridge entries. They were much more optimistic than I had been feeling through round one; they were more hopeful. Certainly, I had bad days and sad days and *very, very mad days*, but I was finally moving beyond the lesson. Now, the expectation for me was to apply it. I had learned that my moods didn't change the outcome; so, I needed to react in better ways. I made a vow to begin to focus on the positive and snap myself out of my doldrums and the many self-pity parties I had been hosting. I went to the gym. I studied harder. I ate better. It really helped to communicate and journal my thoughts to my faithful CaringBridge readers, all of whom consistently provided me with messages of encouragement, support, Bible verses to ponder, prayers and memories that I could hold in my heart. It was tangible support that I could turn to, at any time.

I could put out a message at ten o'clock at night on the CaringBridge page, all alone in my hospital bed; a message chock-full of ranting and raving, frustration and upset, followed up with declarations that I was *done* with treatment, drained emotionally and end my piece by threatening to throw in the white towel on my never-ending saga. Then, I would fall asleep, spent. Miracle of miracles, by morning, I would open the site and I would read perfectly targeted and uplifting words of support, encouragement and love, written just to me. The messages on the CaringBridge site sustained me and lifted the black clouds over me. Reading on my CaringBridge page that Abby was online that morning and understood how I felt and that she wished she could sing me a song to brighten my day, or that Mom had read my entry and agreed with me and wanted me to eat my asparagus and wear my blue striped boots the next time it rained were symphonic words to my ears. Contemplating the poetry and the Bible verses that were quoted on my page and knowing that so many were climbing with me up this mountain of treatment, served to broaden my outlook and my spirits, in so many positive ways. It strengthened me to read that I was strong and that I was fighting the good fight and that the people that I loved and cared about all admired and loved me, right back.

Now that my attitude had changed somewhat, I found myself open to meeting many new and interesting people. They were seemingly coming out of the woodwork. Some would quietly listen to my story; others shared theirs. Many just hugged me and most told me that they were praying for me. One or two special people even taught me how to pray. One particular woman, Coach Mary, of the lacrosse team at college may not know it, but she led me to believe that I was worthy of believing in and her words got me to thinking—maybe she was right—maybe, I did have a story to tell, that would, as I had heard from her, *touch others with just one word.* But that is not all that Coach Mary did for me. Coach Mary taught me how to pray-out-loud-pray. Her kind guidance showed me how to go beyond just reciting some long ago memorized and half-forgotten verse. Coach Mary helped me to find the words that I could use to openly pray for myself and for my specific needs. The student was ready.

I needed these platitudes. They were all like gifts to me. I was running on empty, with scissors in my hands, beside a wet pool. I needed to surround myself with these new people that were surreptitiously appearing in my life. Their outlook and the uplifting words they shared with me made my heart glad. I *did* want to make a difference. I had spent all of my life planning to be *that change* in people's lives and now, hearing and reading that I *was* that beacon, and that I was making *that difference* completely turned my way of thinking and my outlook on my situation around. I was beginning to finally realize that, just like Mom had written, *crisis is just exactly the invitation a miracle needs.* I was rounding the bend and beginning to see that I was not as far away, as I thought I was, from witnessing my own miracle. It was becoming abundantly clear to me now how important it was to be kind and open to the many new people that were entering my life: doctors, nurses, teachers, and strangers alike, because, really, I just never knew when I might be meeting an angel. My life was becoming full of them.

Don't get me wrong. MaDee here. I continued to do battle with the dragons and the demons; I did not feel heroic. I did not want the pressure of being the example of a gracious, benevolent and beautiful young cancer patient. I wanted my life back, normal in every way possible; I would be remiss in denying that. But, somewhere along the lines of the CaringBridge prayers and positive messages, I began to feel the mustard seeds of transformation. My support system was uplifting me. As I headed into the next grueling stage of treatment, I was beginning to believe my mom, who had always said, "MaDee, there are two ways you can look at this. You can look at it as though nothing were a miracle, or, you *could* view it as if everything were a miracle." Mom was right. I wanted to be that miracle.

I felt the prayers; I really did. I wanted my dreams and hopes to remain alive. I finally let others carry me, so that I could rest. I was so tired and I had come to the point that I was no longer able to bear the burden of this disease, by myself. I was done with shouldering this painful process and trying to be the one who could stand up, unaided, against the cancer. I made it my motto to say the words from the poem, "*Footprints in the Sand*" over and over again, to myself. I knew that I was being carried, for the first time in a very long time and that I could finally allow myself to rest. My mom gently reminded me that *Jesus slept.*[1] I needed to rest, too.

My friends, my family and the new people that were coming into my life, after I was diagnosed for the second time, were as much a part of the healing and transformation that I was about to experience, as the medicines were. It was because of my immense circle of friends that I truly came into the belief that I was safe and that I would be protected. I finally allowed others to take the lead and walk ahead of me for awhile, so that I could take the time to get the rest that I needed. As I headed into transplant, almost one year to the day, from diagnosis, I leaned on *my people* and I felt positive. It really was a good thing everyone circled the wagons because this dog and pony show was just getting started. I was about to face the hardest part of this journey and, this time, it wasn't going to have anything to do with cancer.

---

1 See Mark 4:38

Chapter Fifteen

Whack-A-Mole

Life was beginning to take on the characteristics of a carnival game and I was the mole. Over the next six months I began to feel that no matter what plans were made for my treatment, something was going to stand over me with a black mallet and hammer the idea and my life, into a cavernous pit. The cancer was laughing at me and at all that I was throwing at it, not to mention that my treatments and the hospital admissions were getting longer, more repetitious, and, seemingly futile. Just when I would fend off the growth of one tumor, another one would rear its ugly head or reappear in a new place inside me. I had multiple reoccurring attacks from the dragon, every one of which was hitting me from a new direction. Nothing was working and with every day that passed I was actually getting further away from transplant, instead of closer to my goal.

The vast community of people that were leading me up this mountain probably never really knew just how hard it was going to be to keep their hands on my back and push me up and around the boulders that kept falling into the road, in front of me. The idea that I was running out of options and time was forefront in my mind now. My fear was growing like an uncontained Arizona wildfire and I felt like I had gotten caught in the backdraft. I had less than a few options to tame the beastly creature. I needed God to not only hear my loud and long prayers and free me from my fear, but I also needed Him to keep my bone marrow clear of disease and, what's more, *if* He had the time, I needed Him to take away the symptoms that were beginning to interrupt my time with Him.

My prayer list of needs was great and growing by leaps and bounds. Mom and Abby continued to remind me that His power was bigger than all of my needs combined and that He had me in the palm of His hand.

By mid April, just after receiving months of a strenuous chemo treatment called ICE, and, just before scan time, there were again *symptoms* that left little doubt in my mind that *it* had returned, for the third time. Cancer patients can usually tell their doctors that they have relapsed, even before the scans do. Dr. Douvas asked me if I was expecting bad results when we talked and I nodded my head, *yes*. A few short days later I found out that I was right. *It* was back, again.

In fact, my scans revealed that not only was the beast spitting in the face of the new treatment, drinking the poisonous toxins like Kool-Aid, he was growing rapidly. My disease was finding fertile ground now in my tailbone and I was beginning to feel a new spot in my chest. Not only was I trying to whack a mole, I was playing the carnival game in the dark, with no idea where the pest would pop up next and no way to see him, when he did.

I was losing ground. Already, we were headed into late spring and with each new scan and each new symptom, I was that much further away from the transplant that was designed to save me. I was running out of time and more importantly my options were dwindling. I was hitting walls of self doubt that were larger and more powerful than any roadblock the cancer had ever thrown in my path. I was losing faith in my treatments, at a greater rate than the cancer was growing.

The doctors quickly came up with a new plan, called IVEG, and I was told that I needed to start straightaway. There was just one problem. I could not do it. I had done enough. I was tired. I was completely put off, put upon and put out at continuously being slapped in the face by this beast. I did not want to continue treatment. More than anything, I just wasn't ready. I told everyone I could tell that I was upset, angry, frustrated and full of questions. I had lost my hope and any belief in the medication. Scientifically, in my mind, nothing was working and I really did not want another round of useless chemo. I had, by this time, ingested or infused wheelbarrows full of drugs and, despite having come this far, chemo was the one thing I just could not ever get used to. I was tired of being called *strong* and reading about strength in the face of adversity. *Wasn't two bouts enough?* Doubt was hitting at speeds in excess of 200 miles per hour. My third relapse was enough to knock me completely off the tracks.

My family was adamant that I needed to re-enter the hospital and begin treatment, which made me feel incredible guilt at even thinking about not proceeding. I was begged to continue. Friends talked to me about uphill climbs, but I could hear the rocks slipping off the cliff and I was the one standing on the edge, alone, looking over it. I absolutely hated the thought of more chemo, longer hospital stays and the plan to use *sister* drugs, when their *brothers* had not worked well, if at all, in the first place. I was not insane to want to stop treatment; I would have been insane to believe that any of the medicines were going to cure me.

Granted, I did not want to give up completely; I just wanted to stop this treatment and go somewhere else and try something new. I had the overriding feeling, in every pore of me, that I was just going through the motions with these drugs and I knew, deep in that pit of my stomach, that they were not going to work. I had lost all confidence in this chemo. I had no idea what would work for me and just like all the others who were with me at this carnival of horrors—namely my life—I wanted to try my hand at hitting the moles that popped up, too.

If the truth were to be told, I was *furious* that the cancer had come back, for a third time. I had accepted the notion that I was sick, reluctantly, when I received the first diagnosis and I was compliant with the orders for treatment. I dealt with the second relapse in better and more productive ways and I made it a priority to do everything that I was asked to do, in nicer ways and with a better attitude. But now, looking back over those two rounds, I was heartbroken that I had missed the *college experience*, spending all of my time running to catch up on missed classes and IVs chock full of chemo. I was fraught with an overwhelming sense of unfairness at cancer striking me or any other child or young adult, at such a tender age, not only once, or twice, but three times. I couldn't do the normal things my friends were doing. Instead, I got up each day, ate a breakfast of pills, went to class in pain, came home, struggled with nausea, took more pain medication, barfed, slept fitfully and then got up the next day to try to get ready for more chemo. It would have been easier to live my life as a cow, chewing my own cud. I was sick and tired of being sick and tired.

I was just miserable. I was still feeling depressed and I began to wonder if the antidepressants that I had been taking were being counteracted by some of the treatment medications I was receiving, because if not—they were not working—and I needed to see about an increase in the dose. I wanted anything but what I had going on inside my head and, more, I wanted to feel better. I became especially interested in trying some alternative treatments—anything new—and my mom researched constantly, trying to assuage me. I had horrible premonitions and even worse nightmares. I was saddened by my parent's divorce and I still felt heart-broken and missed Chris, in the worst possible way. I could not concentrate on my school assignments. I felt alone, spent and used up. I wanted a surgeon to come in and literally cut out all the pieces and parts of me that were hurting. I was tired of fighting a losing battle, with now two cancerous places in my chest, a growing area in my lymph nodes and a new tumor around my tailbone. I was being eaten alive, from the inside out. I was starting to believe that it would feel better to die.

My mom was terrified at the relapse but more, at my reaction to it, and when we get scared, I take a nap and she reads. She came up with new ideas and new places we could go, to get second opinions and to see what other options were out there for me. Mom and Abby prayed, unceasingly, for me. They talked for hours, wrote close friends and family and begged them to do what they could do to lift my spirits and to convince me to continue treatment. They pleaded with me. They begged.

Mom came up with a bribe. If I would continue treatment, just as the doctors were prescribing, she *promised* me, that we could then seek a second opinion and start to do some of the things I wanted to do.

Mom encouraged me to focus on only the day in front of me. She single-handedly *brought the Word to me*, with her incredible faith and her sense that God was awesome, in control and that He would heal me, if only I would believe. She reminded me, as often as I would listen, that God had this whole thing under His control, and, that absolutely nothing was too big for Him to handle. My mom was a veritable rock of strength during this time, and she did everything in her power to pick up the proverbial white towel of surrender that I was throwing on the floor. She reminded me, countless times, that I might not be seeing the whole picture. But, she knew better than to overwhelm me with her ideas, so she called on others to lead me back into the *kick butt* positive attitude I had had for the last year. She plodded through her fears, concerns, doubts and her worries and she remained encouraging, upbeat and positive, in the face of incredible odds and the horrendous sadness that she was witnessing in her daughter and in her own personal life.

Abby rallied too, in the most unbelievable of ways. She would come to the hospital in the evening, after work and she would climb right up in the bed beside me, always with that certain smile on her face that would soothe me in an instant. We would watch movies or lay in the bed and talk ourselves silly as they played on the screen in front of us. Abby always had an amusing tale to tell, often at her own expense, and I knew, looking forward to her visits, that when Chrissy came, she would come bearing me *kissths* and she would make my heart glad, as only she could do.

Abby and my mom literally picked me up and held me together by my bootstraps. They took the pieces and parts of my splitting head, my broken heart and my tattered and worn body that the cancer had aimlessly strewn about and day after long day, jagged edge by jagged edge, they mended and smoothed the pieces of my fighting spirit back together again. Together, they replaced my broken dreams with new ones and sealed my heartache with their love. While there wasn't much that they could think to do about my medical condition, they even came up with a plan about that, too.

New York had always enticed me, with its neon signs and its tall buildings full of revolving doors and television stars. I loved big cities and one of my dreams had always been to see a Broadway play. I had always imagined myself as Julia Roberts, walking down the city streets, shopping in the finest of stores, eating at the fanciest of restaurants and then, *dressed to the nines*, hailing a taxi to the theatre, where I would step out, in my heels and fancy frock, to buy a ticket to a show—a Broadway show. An evening such as this was number two on my bucket list. Somehow, the idea of watching a play, of settling into the world of play-acting—where all of my dreams *could* come true—living and in color, was enticing to me. Flying on a plane for the first time, shopping at Tiffany's and buying a new Coach purse, staying in a fine hotel and eating in a local eatery, followed by "Wicked" on Broadway seemed like the perfect plan. Just thinking about such a fantasy trip started to lift my sagging soul and bolster my sad spirits.

Mom had made arrangements for me to get a second opinion in New York at Memorial Sloan-Kettering Cancer Institute. It was purely at my request, and, as part of the deal, I had agreed with her to complete the first round of an aggressive new treatment in Virginia. Further, she wanted me to quit thinking about non-medical and whacky alternatives and, more importantly, she made me promise to dispense with words having anything to do with *stopping* my treatment. This was a woman who did not mince words. I would have three weeks before the next round was scheduled to look at my options and it was then, that we would travel to New York. I agreed to the new plan and admitted myself to the hospital.

This particular ICE treatment was tough. I had never before needed blood products to raise dangerously low hemoglobin levels, but this time my counts were plummeting. Still, after I got out of the hospital, I remained focused on my life and some of the new attitude returned. I was going to the gym, studying and, when I had to, resting. I did everything I could do to keep my life on track and I looked forward to our trip to New York. Despite my mom's admonitions, I started taking some supplements to cleanse my body of toxins.

I began to feel vestiges of hope return again. Hope arrived just before we left on a jet plane, for New York. Hope and I were new companions and inseparable, for a time. The idea of going for a second opinion was just what I needed. I wanted to find, in the Big Apple, a plan that I could participate in for my wellness and a plan that I felt like had a *coon's chance* of working. I thought New York would be just the place to get it. My doctors locally were in complete agreement with my quest and they supported me. Just knowing that my home team was honoring how I felt about my disease and having them understand how much I needed to try something new, was the recipe for the return of some semblance of positivity in my outlook. I was finally going to do something on my own that was aggressive and I had visions of finally beating down my adversary. Leaving for New York, on a jet plane, brought hope and my fighting spirit back. I was determined. I was going to get that mole.

Chapter Sixteen

The Concrete Jungle

I had to try to get better. Nothing about me was about being sick. It felt great to be discharged from the hospital in Virginia and I felt perfect contentment, bound for New York. Sitting high up in that silver bird up in the sky, with my head resting on Abby's shoulder, I knew Billy Preston had gotten it right; I felt like a bird up in the sky.

Everything looks different, every single day, in New York City and my first trip there was fabulous. It was the kind of trip that makes you want to come back, again and again. Times Square in early summer is teaming with newness and everything felt so *alive*. It was not hot enough yet in the season to dodge steam and spewing hydrants in the street. It was still cool and I enjoyed walking almost everywhere, or blanketing Abby and myself for a tricycle ride around Central Park. The *concrete jungle* really never sleeps and that excitement was contagious. I was up at dawn to see Robin Roberts and the Good Morning America crew. I was exuberant standing in the crowd to hear Lionel Ritchie sing in *the* Park and, nothing makes the metallic taste of chemo disappear faster than a slice of famous Italian pizza, smothered in mozzarella cheese.

When you are in New York and especially when you enter the gigantic doors of the Memorial Sloan-Kettering Cancer Center, you had better know where you are going or act like you do. Security is tight. Finally inside the famed treatment center, we walked among scores of people seeking treatment, until we found the area where we were requested to sit and wait to meet with the doctor.

After making brief introductions, I gave this new doctor my history. *MaDee has cancer.* Then, we got the news that I knew was coming and that I was somehow, expecting, but nevertheless, did not want to hear. The doctor told us that it looked like I would need one more round of chemo and then, hopefully, I could proceed to transplant. By now the words, *one more round of chemo,* were as old to me as the hollow tinkering sound in a street beggar's tin cup. This was not what I had flown all this way to hear.

I sat on the exam table and I listened to the doctor, so hoping to find an alternative to chemo and to a transplant, but I really didn't know what that would entail. Nothing about my disease made any sense to me. Some people had tiny amounts of disease that never responded to therapy; yet others, receiving the same medicine for a ton of disease, walked away with a clean bill of health. My cancer wasn't just *bad* anymore; it was off the charts, horrible. Soon, I doubted anyone was going to be able to find any normal cells in me, at all. I wanted some new research, a non-FDA approved set of drugs that I could take that would miraculously cure me of this latest relapse. I asked the doctor in New York for *the magic pill,* as if he was a wizard and could grant me my wish. I needed a drug I could take, every day, for the rest of my life, if need be, to cure me. I wanted the doctor in New York to *prescribe normal* for me and watch me go fill it. While everyone that day wanted the very same thing for me, such a treatment simply did not exist.

I did not leave empty handed. I did come away from New York with one important gift. The New York doctor *applauded* my Virginia doctors. In essence, he rekindled the flames of my desire to return home, assuring me that I was being cared for by the best our country had to offer in the way of hematologists and oncologists. I already knew this, but having him reassure me that I was being cared for in those terms was comforting, somehow. I was told that *had I been his patient* from the beginning, he would have done the exact same things and presented me with similar options. This was salve to my fears and I am equally sure that it took the pressure off the hometown team to perform the miracles I was seeking, when, in fact, there were none.

I laid it all on the table and *getting it all out and out of the way* was gratifying. I told the doctor that I was hesitant now to pursue further treatment. I explained to him in detail, that I had felt, for some time now, that these last few treatment modalities had been a complete waste of my precious time. The doctor listened to me and then he explained, carefully, the difference between good treatments and greater disease process. He laid the blame for this feeling right where it belonged—at cancer's feet—and not at the hands of the medicine or the heart of the physicians. I was fighting a formidable opponent and despite the best of treatments, this was unfortunately, not good enough to slay the dragon. What I had received was as good as it could get, at this stage in medical advancements. I came to realize, sitting in that room, that there was *never* going to be a secret as to what was going to save me. No one held the golden key, which meant that I couldn't screw this whole thing up, even if I tried.

I also heard the same old song and dance about clean scans, here in this hospital, too. Absolutely everything I wanted to do hinged on clean scans, again, but this time, the stakes were raised. No clean scans—no transplant—pure and simple. My body *had* to be clear and clean of cancer cells for me to have even a chance of accepting the transplanted cells. No one here in New York or back home in Virginia wanted me to fall victim to the selfsame invasive cancer cells, after a transplant. There were few, if any, *do-overs,* after such a last ditch effort to save me. No one wanted to put me into life-threatening treatment, without the best chance of recovery, and even the slightest vestige of a cancer cell in me could skew the results in favor of the beast.

I asked the hard questions in New York. I was ready to know what exactly would happen to me if I chose not to proceed with the second round of chemo, which, at this point was a week behind schedule. I received the hard answers, kindly. I was told that if I was to forego the next round, it would be *then* that I must be willing to look at the first round as a complete waste of my time. At this point the first round could be considered *a win,* and not a waste of my time. If I walked away from the best that research and modern medical advancements had to offer—if I turned my back on them now—I was told that I would be certain to suffer defeat. Now, I was the one that was going to have to make the decision of whether or not to forfeit the game.

The conversation and the tone of the physician was laced with a feeling of confidence that I could beat this, because, as he pointed out, I was young, strong, active and really, quite healthy overall, aside from the cancer. The consensus was that I had a *fighting chance.* All the things that I had been doing, such as continuing with my school, counseling and working out at the gym—the continual push to lead as normal a life as possible—were, for him, strong indicators that I wanted to continue to fight and that I just might make it.

I was given a list of options. I was told that the medicinal cupboard was full of drugs, that while experimental, could trick the cancer into submission, should I need them, in order to get to transplant, in remission. I was reassured that if my next scans were not clear, there would be a plan B, C, D and maybe even a plan E.

The conversation went to the places that I had never gone, at least not in front of Mom, Dad and Abby, and directly with the doctors at home. Perhaps I didn't go there because they cared so much about me, or, maybe it was because I was not ready to hear the answers. But, this time, I finally asked the age old question: *Am I going to die*?

The doctor was able to gently lay out on the table for me the idea of life goals, once I managed to choke up the remaining parts of my query. What I really hoped to hear was what were my chances for *living.* In his words and in response to my feeble attempt at this question, I was told that it was going to be entirely up to me to decide what my life goals were. If I wished to stop treatments, finish college and be as normal as possible, then I was probably looking at a lifespan of six months to a year; my cancer was just that aggressive. *However*, if I wanted to be around to see the next five years, he opined that I probably ought to do more. And on and on it went, as he laid out my odds. I remember hearing Mom remark, almost to herself, as we walked up the street after the meeting, "Hmmm, he never seemed to mention the idea that really, MaDee, none of us knows—no one on this Earth could *possibly* know—the plans God has for you and how powerful are His ways." Mom left New York unchanged in her beliefs and I followed along behind her, thinking about changing mine.

Sitting with Abby in the hotel room on the bed together, later that night, my sister and I had a deep and long heart-to-heart talk. We spoke about the last piece of news the physician had given me, which was that I had to have a donor for the transplant and in finding that donor, *time was of the essence*. No longer could I harvest my own cells, as we had planned all along; the disease was too foolhardy and wickedly aggressive, growing from a Stage 2 to a Stage 4, with three relapses, in one year's time. A donor needed to be found, *now*. I could no longer hope, with the aid of medicine, to harvest my own cells and save myself. Abby listened to me, quietly, and she let me process my thoughts on my own, but I could tell that the wheels were churning in her head.

I had never had my blood typed for a donor match, because I was always thinking that the treatments would work, or, worst case, that I would provide my own cells for transplant. There was a process whereby the doctors could *clean up* my own cells and replace them in the transplant, but now I knew, from further reading and from the conversations with the staff at Sloan that my own cells were not a candidate for this process. Now, if I did not find a match from within my circlc in a huge hurry, I would be faced with searching the nationwide donor base. A search like that, took weeks—sometimes months—and oftentimes turned up nothing. I didn't have the luxury of that amount of time to look for a suitable match and I certainly could not risk a failed attempt at a match if I did find one.

I had agreed to have blood drawn that day, before I left Sloan, and the doctor had suggested that Abby be set up for the next day. She was introduced as my first and last hope for a related donor match. I can't even imagine what it must have felt like for Abby to have about twenty-four *seconds* to react to the news that she was going to walk the gauntlet with me and that all the odds were being put against her, as being exactly the blood type that I needed. The doctor had told us that percentage wise, the chances of my blood and Abby's being perfectly synchronized, were less than what we needed them to be, by a very formidable degree.

So, Abby and I talked about the fact that we had yet another race to run, eleven more weeks before school started again, and this time, things had to go according to plan. We *really* needed Abby's cells to match mine and we both knew it, but, that's the funny thing about cancer and blood, until those tests were run, no one could see a thing or predict what the results would be. We knew that the chances of Abby being the match that I needed were practically nil. All of a sudden, after hearing all of this news, New York became a jungle of confusion and bright lights and chaos and we just wanted to go home. There was no place like home. I sat up on the hotel room bed, looked at Abby and without saying a word I grabbed the phone and I dialed my doctor's office in Virginia. Abby and I had just made an appointment for Round Two.

I was beginning to learn, as all cancer patients do, that I could not plan. All I could do was wait on my body to cooperate. The New York doctors had made me see that while I did not want to continue to be treated, it was something that I had to do, if I wanted to take the long range view and live longer than a year's time. I was now in a great deal more pain—more than ever before. The tumor in my tailbone bothered me at night, enough to need rather significant pain medication. Thankfully, at least my thoughts had turned the corner and were not plaguing me with anxiety over what should be done and causing me additional reasons for sleeplessness.

Time marched on and I spent it waiting to recover after the chemo and jumping every time the phone rang, hoping to receive word about Abby's blood match. As was my custom, I filled my days with a great deal of work, sprinkled with short vacations with my mom and I was able to slip away with some friends for short trips, too. It felt good to get out of town and have it be for fun, not an appointment. I loved walking on the beach and feeling the sand in my toes. It had been far too long since I had planned a get-a-way, with Mom or Amanda, and even though these were only short day trips and overnights, I relished every second that I had to recharge. I knew that these day trips just might be some of the last ones with my mom—not because I would never have the chance to go again somewhere with her—but, because I wanted to begin to think about travel in terms of living on my own again and making my own plans with friends.

The pain was worsening in my tailbone and left leg. It came with me, wherever I went. It had become constant, numbing and acute, all at the same time. It was difficult to allow the calendar days to pass me by, not knowing if Abby was a match or if the chemo I had agreed to was working and all of us, no matter where we were, added pleas for patience to our nightly prayers.

Soon, it was late June, and *scan time again.* This particular scan, if it was clean, was my ticket to transplant, in New York. We had been informed just prior to the scan date, that Abby was a ten point match for transplant, which became the wind beneath my sails, served to rejuvenate us all, and, of course, was cause for great happiness. The doctors were only hoping that Abby's blood was a seven point match for me; this was the best they were expecting. Hearing that she came in a *perfect ten point match* was the miracle we had all prayed for. There was no other way to describe it.

Now, everything hinged on my scans and as was so often the case, once we got the results, we found out that the cancer would, again, not cooperate. While my scans were better, they were not good enough. The new edict was that I had to go through *yet another round of chemo*, rest for three weeks and let them collect my sister's cells. I would have another chemo cocktail and then—finally—proceed to transplant.

I imploded! This new calendaring of the transplant and this new set of chemo would interfere with my one and only goal of graduation from Roanoke College in December. I refused to discuss it with anyone and I slunk away to lick my wounds, scaring my family half to death. I thought about trying to get a third opinion in Chicago at the Cancer Treatment Center of America. I wrote about it. I considered postponing the schedule even more, so that I could graduate with my class. I threatened to do nothing and, most of all, I thought about how inordinately *mad* I was.

My mom told me later that she called my doctor, fraught with anxiety, about what she could do to calm me down. The doctor was gentle, but matter of fact with her, and he told her that I needed to understand, in no uncertain terms, that

I was presently looking at the only real window of opportunity available to me. This time Mom was remembering a different doctor—the one in New York—that had shared a story with us about another patient—one who waited—and the ending was not a good one. The cold hard truth was this: Hodgkin's lymphoma was not going to wait on MaDee Jane Nicole Boxler. I had to meet it head on and on its terms.

Dr. Douvas knew me, inside and out, by now, and he was an expert in reading me. He made the right choice in deciding to wait a day, after speaking with my mom, before he made a call to me. I had the night to think, calm down and I had the next day, with its accompanying pain, to bring me quickly and squarely back to reality. After talking calmly with Dr. Douvas, I signed on for yet another five day round of chemo. We planned to set me up to return to New York, after my Virginia admission and begin the process of gathering Abby's cells.

Once again, I did as I was told. And, I took every sort of medication they would give me for the tailbone pain and then I asked for seconds. The doctors were becoming increasingly concerned with the duration and the level of pain that I was experiencing and they thought perhaps it was the tumor pressing on the nerves in my leg and bladder. They had ruled out biopsy injury. This left one assumption: *it* was probably growing, *again.* I had such little time, such few precious pain-free moments and I was running scared, living on Vicodan, four times a day.

More changes. More not normal. More pain. More likely progression of disease. But, my school had agreed to allow me to finish my degree online, which, while not ideal, was necessary and I was gratified that they were so willing to work with me. Abby had her testing done on our second visit to New York and I went with her, to meet my transplant team.

Our return to Virginia however, brought more and more hoops that I had to jump through. The MRI of my tailbone had shown an increase in the tumor—*again*. After all of the new chemo and all of the additional admissions, we were told that the chemotherapy was no longer working. I had missed the transplant boat, again.

I was then prescribed a drug therapy known as MOPP. The only thing good about it was that, aside from a few injections, it was finally, an at-home chemo, with no admissions. Once again, I was told that the scans *had* to show improvement, and if they did, it would be off to New York for transplant. If not, then, well, no one really said. I held onto the thought that this treatment would work and I finished up my injections for the first cycle of MOPP. The symptoms and pain were lessening and everyone was in agreement that my time had finally come to head to the Big Apple, in September, finalize the details of transplant, sign off on an admission and then wait for Abby's healthy cells to be implanted in me. I had just caught a proverbial wave!

Chapter Seventeen

Three, Four, Shut the Door

Where was my Gilda when I needed her? I wanted my dreams to be granted by the good witch from the East and do away forever with the nasty, wicked witch from the West, who had her sights on forever banishing me to the cold and banal world of lymphoma. Ah, if only life were like a fairy tale...become a princess, meet a handsome prince, fall in love and live, *happily ever after*, all the while shopping at Coach, on Fifth Avenue. But *all the King's horses and all the King's men* couldn't seem to put MaDee back together again. I was falling apart, literally, at the seams and on the sidewalks and streets of New York, just outside of the massive institution I needed to treat me. I was going to need a miracle to gain entrance through the castle walls.

Just after my twenty-second birthday, Abby and I traveled to New York, saw the transplant rooms and met with the team of administrators, social workers and doctors. We looked at accommodations and I fell in love with Hope Lodge, a place where I could heal, during the weeks after my transplant. I underwent more testing and while the staff seemed to feel cautiously optimistic that I would proceed to transplant, the fact remained that clean scans and a clear bone marrow test would be the deciding factor. I traveled back south, having caught New York's spirit of optimism. I should have known better.

I really believed that this time everything was coming up roses and finally, I was the gal picked to be the princess on the parade float. I had less pain; I had done exactly what my doctors had asked me to do and I was finished with the MOPP therapy. I was feeling so much better, with more energy to do all the things that I loved to do. I had the right attitude and I had the backing of what I considered to be the best in the nation, ready to whisk me into transplant. But for the scans.

The results showed *more growth* of the tumor in my tailbone which meant that I was not a candidate for transplant. There was now, nothing further that anyone could do for me, in Virginia, by way of standard and nonstandard chemotherapies. But, Dr. Douvas did *not* give up. He quickly obtained my permission to consult with his colleagues across the country, but it was now our thought that my best chance to gain a grip on the tumors was to return to New York and look at experimental drugs. If I thought that I was scared to go to New York for transplant, thinking that I was now going to have to go to the *land of opportunity* for a last-ditch clinical effort to save me was over the top, shake me from the bottom up, drag me to my knees, scary.

Needless to say, we jumped right on the bus, thinking it was better to ride this one, than to be hit by it. Mom, Abby, Dad and I packed our bags. *If this was how it was going to play out, well then, game on—bring it.* I can remember thinking that at this point, I just wanted the doctors to give me a kitchen sink full of chemo drugs, if that was what it was going to take, to get me to transplant. I was now ready to ingest anything. Forget easy and leisurely; give me quick and brutal. *Let's get this show on the road.* I was so floored by the number of dead end roads we had traversed; I wanted to start down another one, immediately.

A couple of days and delays later, sometime in late October, after booster injections to stimulate my marrow to produce enough blood cells to be treated, I was one step away from a trial drug used for non Hodgkin's lymphoma patients, developed with the hope that if it was used on a Hodgkin's patient, *me*, perhaps it would trick the cells and stop their progression. I received the drug in New York and I returned home, carrying it like a challis, in my hands. I was so hopeful that this drug would be the magic potion that would set the carriage wheels of my transplant in motion.

Actually, the drug was not too bad. My hair stayed curly and on my head; I did not suffer from the pangs of nausea. My counts remained stable. I did not have to have the painful Neulasta shots. I should have known that something was amiss—this treatment was way too tolerable. I should have questioned whether or not it was working. In short order, I would have gladly researched that subject and asked more questions, if the answers would have done anything to stop the pain in my tailbone.

I hurt. In the worst way possible, I hurt. I could not find a medicine strong enough for the pain in the lower half of my body. To make the situation worse, my legs had stopped carrying me the way that I needed them to. They felt like steel anchors, plunged deeply into quicksand. My bladder and my bowels were leaking, which meant that I now needed help with the most basic of functions. I wasn't a five-year-old child anymore; I was an infant. I could think of nothing worse than spending my life in diapers. I remember telling Mom, as she bent to clean the drippage that had come down the back of my left leg and landed on the floor, "Mom, I cannot do this. I just cannot do *this*."

I wrote some of my concerns, in my journal on the CaringBridge site, and I left the remainder in my personal papers.

> I have also had the motor function (not sure if that's how you say it) issues come. For example, my legs feel as if they weigh (2,000,000) pounds and I can('t) go upstairs without pulling myself up and having someone behind me and I can't stand on my tippy toes. These are just a few of the changes I will share. These changes might seem small in the everyday (w)orld, but to me they are huge. For those of you who know me well, you know that I hate this!

I couldn't sleep. I couldn't eat. I couldn't walk. I couldn't stop my hands from shaking to even take a sip of coffee and now I was losing control of my cleanliness. I spent my days in constant pain and I couldn't break free of the agonizing tremors and the numbness that alternated with sharp, shooting pangs in my legs. The pain was so intense that it felt like a five-foot warehouse fan set on high blowing against me, making it hard to breathe. I was emotional now, *all* of the time. I was on the edge of needing an IV of morphine, in the hospital, constantly. To make matters worse, I felt a huge spot protruding from my chest...*again.* This spot was the largest it had ever been and took up practically the entire area of my palm. It felt hard, like a mourning dove. I knew that the monster was *feasting* on me now.

At this point I was begging for prayer and I was pleading for relief. People were taking my petition to the Wailing Wall, in Jerusalem and prayer vigils were being held. My grandparents set up mass for me. There were many fund raisers. None of this journey had come cheap and everyone wanted to see me. My friends and my family were overcome with a feeling of helplessness and everyone who knew me was storming the Heavens, begging for mercy, but in the same breath, urging me to stay strong. My mom put out an intercessory Email request, asking people to pray on my behalf, whenever they might think of me. Her words were simple, sweet-sounding and, very much to the point. *God, you are so awesome. Thank you for healing MaDee.*

This reaction that I was having was not a good one to the trial drug and the doctors pulled me from the study. New York had now turned me away; their cabinets and drawers of experimental medicines, in the infant stages of success, were completely bare. Not even Old Mother Hubbard had anything in her cupboard and because I had been placed on the crème de la crème of promising treatment modalities, anything else that they could concoct would have been laughable.

Somehow, thanks to Dr. Douvas, the goal remained the same—transplant—but, we had to move quickly. I was sent to meet with a physician in Maryland, at Johns Hopkins, and after our initial meeting, my hopes for a ticket to wellness were thrashed. Hopkins had a treatment protocol that might help me, but it would take over two weeks to work and having just turned twenty-two years old, staring at the aggressive cancer that was bearing down on me, everyone realized that I just did not have that kind of time.

Once again, my steadfast and knowledgeable home team designed a plan. Awhile back, when the pain was unrelenting, Dr. Douvas had placed me on steroids as a way to reduce the inflammation and to relieve the nerve compression causing me so much discomfort. What wasn't expected was that we were seeing results that seemed to indicate that something had turned on the light switch inside of me and gotten the monster's attention. He seemed to be retreating a bit. It was Dr. Douvas' thinking that *maybe, just maybe,* I had been primed and I was also now perhaps going to prove to be responsive to some new-old variations of chemo I had already tried. It was a completely novel and aggressive idea to me, but since I was hanging by a thread of options, I had little choice but to think that he might just be correct. I *was* finally exhibiting positive signs of decreased involvement, so, maybe I might meet with success with this new idea, too. God bless this man, for sticking by me and for consistently putting on his thinking cap for me, every single day.

Dr. Douvas wanted to admit me immediately and get another five day chemo on board. He had the idea, as I understood it, that he would wean me off of the steroids, slowly, in the hopes that my pain would not return with this slow ride to cessation of a drug, that while it lessened the pain for me, was not without significant side effects, namely moodiness, almost to the point of psychosis, weight gain, fluid retention and an insatiable appetite, not to mention pancreatic and other organ concerns. After weaning me from the steroids, it was our hope that I could then take the necessary steps to get to Hopkins. We crossed our fingers and our toes that I had outwitted the gigantic ape on my back and hoped that I had just bought myself fourteen days of time.

Dr. Douvas did not get *one bit of lip* from me. I knew now, without him really coming out and saying it, that I had no choice but to acquiesce and that his plan was my best, and, frankly, just about my final option. More than at any other point in time, I was willing to do anything that he told me to do, without question. *If you want me to jump off a cliff, I will do it.* I completely relinquished the stronghold that I had maintained on how I believed my life and my treatment should be played out. I knew that Dr. Douvas had my best interests at heart and I knew that this scene was one in which I was not going to be the understudy. I had to jump up on the stage, listen to the player more intently and I had to, most importantly, *follow his lead.* MaDee was no longer in control. I had finally learned, on a fair and cold November Monday that there was a script and that I needed to follow it.

It started out like any other ordinary Monday; as ordinary as any other day had been lately, with thoughts that opened like window blinds on the aggressive and now seriously life-threatening cancer that was eating me alive. I dealt with trying to gain the upper hand on the pain that, while it plagued me overnight, was assuaged by sleep. Having skipped a dose of narcotic meant that I had allowed the pain to get ahead of me and playing catch up was no fun. For breakfast I threw up, took a nap and tried to eat again, sometime later. I had constant thoughts about these horrible, satanic-like tumors and masses feasting inside of me, as if they were playing out right before me on *Law and Order* or *CSI*, on the television screen. This show of horrors lasted through lunch which promptly came up the same way it went down.

I took a nap sometime later that afternoon and then, I packed my bag, preparing for my upcoming admission. I would be gone for six days, instead of the usual five this time, so I needed a few extra things in the suitcase that stood always upright and packed in my room. I was hoping, in my good moments, that the treatment would shrink my cancer a bit, before the trial of pills at Hopkins. I was praying and waiting for that one minute, in this next round, when I could feel the spot in my chest start to shrink. I was almost begging for the very precise instant when I would feel the pain in my sacrum subside, enough that I could catch my breath. I was making a few good promises to the Man upstairs. *If you will just let me live....* I spent the whole day packing, praying and fasting.

I was, as usual, emotional and upset, even though I was my typical, rather quiet brew of a self. I had such an overriding sense of being *let down.* Life was just not turning out as I had dreamed it would. In fact, not even so much as a crumb of my former self seemed left anywhere underneath the table now. I had more moments when I wanted to *give up.* I was reaching the point when I wanted someone—anyone—to take away my pain; it was all becoming too much for me to bear.

I had nerve involvement that stung the very fibers in the legs that once allowed me to stand. When I sat, I shook uncontrollably. I had no control over my breath, my bowels, my bladder, my bruising or my being and I was constantly banging up against closed doors and walled-off windows, as if in some horrible tornadic whirlpool, destroying me, from the inside out. I was supposed to be the one leading the battle to help heal me and I was face down on the dirt path, frightened, overcome with pain, depression, darkness of spirit and a complete sense of defeat, mixed with the paralyzing thought that I just might be dying.

Chapter Eighteen

Rainy Days And Mondays

It is known as an *haboob*. An haboob is a massive sand storm that comes out of nowhere and strikes, with great and frightening force. It frequently pelts mountainous quantities of sand, with uncanny force, at anyone and anything near its path, at an average speed of sixty miles, per hour. It's an Arabic term for *phenomenon*, and as such, people in the vast regions of Arabia or the deserts and plains of India know to look for its occurrence quite often, during the spring months. It was, therefore, a complete surprise when it hit me, on Nannie's couch, in the middle of a winter's evening, in Virginia.

The spasms of pain were coming in waves now, so strong as to completely deplete any ability I had left to think. It was as if I was somehow transformed into Alice, falling down into the largest and deepest rabbit hole that I had ever seen. I was being pelted by the greatest system of storms ever encountered. I felt like little more than an old and abandoned rag doll, blowing helplessly down the ravine, with debris and wind speeds that would crush me if I hit the walls. It was as if all of my prayers had turned into foreign schemes made in abandoned houses, to see how much more I could tolerate. I had been besieged by this *beast* for so long now and I had nowhere left to turn, and no one could touch me, not even Abby, much less discuss the *idea* of placing their hands on mine. The increased narcotics that I had been given, over the last few weeks, were doing nothing to dull my senses. I was in agony.

Abby had been rubbing me down as I was getting ready for bed; it was something that she had been doing for me, ever since I had become sick. All of a sudden, the slightest touch of her hand became unbearable. I screamed and I begged for *you—someone—anyone*—to take away the pain. I wanted it cut out of the lower half of me, with a chainsaw from the backyard tool shed. In an instant, this journey had become the pinnacle of all that I could tolerate; this cancer had taken hold of me and this frightening scene was more than I could bear and certainly more than my family should ever have to bear witness to. I had reached the end of tolerance and, now, it made more sense for me to die.

My mom, Abby and my grandparents gathered around me in tribal fashion, as if I had been laid out on the recliner in the dimly lit den, offered up for sacrifice, except that there was nothing to celebrate. I groaned and I cried out for help and they stood there, with tears pouring from their eye's, looking down at me. It had taken hours for them to get me into this chair and they knew there was nothing more that they could do for me, except somehow load me into the car and rush me to the Emergency Room, but I adamantly refused to move. The simple act of moving me would have *killed me*. Abby called Dr. Douvas about my pain. I had a new pain patch and I had been able to keep down one Aleve. So, my family then did what they did best: they prayed and in the minutes when they poured their prayers over me, something began to happen. I prayed, too.

I *finally* prayed for myself. I laid there on the recliner and I put myself completely in God's hands. I gave up all of the control. I closed my eyes and I asked God to take the cancer and the pain out of my body. I asked for His complete help.

I surrendered. I knew now that I needed more than I could ever hope to give myself and that God was the only one who could help me. I could not fight this alone, anymore. I could not keep asking for all the things that I thought I needed. I gave my cancer and my pain and my leadership and my control over to God and, *in that moment*, He accepted all of my horrific disease. Moreover, He accepted me and I felt myself fall into His loving arms. For the first time in my life, I felt God holding me and rubbing my back. The pain was completely gone. The storm had passed and the struggle was over. I slept.

Abby tells the story of that Monday night, in her own words:

> After we prayed over MaDee and just before she fell off into a restless sleep, she looked up at us and said, "God is here." After that statement, she closed her eyes, but occasionally, she would open them wide and look at us, terrified, as if we were the ones hurting her. She appeared dazed and extremely confused as she laid there in a half-awake, half-asleep state, not answering my quietly phrased questions. Minutes would pass, after I asked them. She later told me that the only thing she can remember was "...a feeling that I was spinning, in a dark brown room, with a rocking horse in the corner, on a spring-like frame."
>
> MaDee slept off and on, but it was a disgruntled sleep. She talked a great deal and flailed her arms around. None of what

she said or did made any sense to me, at the time. Mom had finally been convinced to go home and I had sent Nannie and Pop back to bed to rest. I had the next day off from work, so I sat in the TV room with the lights off and I watched her shadow in the dim yellow haze filtering from the streetlight, through the curtained window.

At around two o'clock in the morning, MaDee screamed, loudly. Nannie ran out to see what she could do and we gave MaDee more pain medicine. She was delirious and asking us where everyone was, before she finally fell back to sleep. But her slumber was short lived. MaDee, to me, seemed to be fighting someone or something. She was violently punching with her heretofore useless and shaky arms. She was moving her nerve damaged feet in perfect synchronization. She alternated between yelling out, crying profusely and pleading to whatever it was she could see, that we could not.

I watched my baby sister in mortal terror and fear. I was worried that with all of her movement, she was going to hurt herself, sitting up fighting like she was, in the recliner. In all my life, I had never witnessed anything like the sight of my Chrissy in the chair, that dark and lonely night.

I tried for several minutes to wake MaDee. I shook her shoulders with my face close to hers. Finally, she woke up and I was able to convince her to move to the couch. She looked right through me and talked to me as if I was a stranger.

I knew that this was *not the drugs talking.* MaDee had had far more narcotics than she had received that night. She had only managed to receive her pain patch and take one Aleve. Once I got her settled, I laid on the floor beside her restless body on the couch and I watched the rise and fall of her shoulders; I wanted to make sure that she was still breathing. I was petrified and, therefore completely relieved, when morning finally came and MaDee whispered again. She said, simply, “Jesus.”

I remained on the floor, there beside her. She was sleeping peacefully for the first time in months. I quietly read from Dodie Osteen’s book, *Healed of Cancer.* I would read a scripture, look up from my book, watch MaDee, then read some more and weep. I felt this incredible push in my mind to get on the couch and to hold her. I knew that she needed someone *just to hold her.*

I resisted my urges and I argued with myself. *She is sleeping, Abby. You might wake her. It took forever to settle her.* I wanted this overwhelming need I was feeling to hold my Chrissy, to go away. Then, MaDee sat up and asked to go to the bathroom. This was my time. No excuses. No arguing. I got up from the floor and I reached for her. I just held her in my arms. She let us stay like that for a few minutes and she kept asking me the same question, in as many ways as she could think to phrase it. “What happened to me last night?” MaDee remembered nothing more, beyond the family, praying over her.

Abby held me and then she sat with me and she relayed the story of the previous night to me, as she witnessed it. I listened to her, but her words seemed straight out of a movie. This was a story she was telling *me, about me,* and I honestly didn't know how the next scene was going to play out. Things were moving inside of me as I sat there getting used to the absence of pain and as I listened to my sister telling me the tallest tale that I had ever heard. But the interesting thing was—I felt like the person she was describing—almost as if she had witnessed an accident that had taken me from consciousness. When I sat up on the couch, I was confused and rather frustrated that I could not remember what had happened to me, but as I listened to Abby more closely, I knew that something *miraculous* had just occurred. I felt a thousand pounds lighter, sitting on the couch and I felt a sense of peace and a calmness that had eluded me since that fateful day when I was diagnosed. I still had some slight pain, but now, it was entirely manageable.

I knew, in my heart of hearts, that in me there had been a struggle. I could literally feel the physical effects, as if I had taken a back alley body bashing and had lived to tell about it. Some likened my story to Satan fighting Jesus for my soul; some have called it my salvation. Still others gently reminded me that while I was attempting to hold onto my struggles, all by myself, there was a greater Power willing to take it all in His capable hands. As I thought about the story, it certainly seemed like He had apparently done just that.

Until that Monday night, I had not been ready to accept Christ, defeat, cancer or my fate, in much the same way that I was not ready for so many of my prior treatments. I was just *not ready* to change. *Had the teacher just appeared?* I had been selfish and no one knew that better than me. I knew now that there was a reason that I was still alive. It was glaringly apparent that I was *still kickin'*, because God still had a use for me. Obviously, my job was far from over, otherwise, I would not be where I was, going through what I was going through, if not to carry out, in some unknown fashion, His divine plan for my life.

With these brand new thoughts and ideas in the forefront of my mind, my pain started to make some sense. Sure, I still had cancer and that caused pain. Fact of life. A given, but not a God-given pain, beset on me for something that I had chosen to do or not to do. God did not *give me* cancer, anymore than I gave it to myself and He wept right alongside me, when it hurt like it did. Cancer was an earthly disease and while He did not give it to me, He, alone, was the only one capable of completely taking it away, or, He could decide to perform a miracle in my life and let the medicines do it. It was up to Him to see me through.

I had just been healed. In my new way of thinking, I felt serene for the first time since my diagnosis. I had a *place* to put all of my problems and all of my fears. I had a sister that had struggled right alongside me, as I learned to reach out to Jesus and turn all of my cares and troubles over to

Him. Abby could relate to my newfound serenity, in a way that no one else could. She was with me and she saw it; the struggle and the miraculous transformation.

Mom had no doubt about my salvation either. She could immediately tell there had been a dramatic change in me when she came back to the house the next morning. Mom could find a miracle in anything, but now I think she even surprised herself at the fulfillment of her many prayers for me. All of a sudden, all of the healing scriptures she had spoken and set before me to read, made perfect sense to me and we were finally able to talk about them through the weeks ahead. What a glorious moment in time that must have been for Mom.

There was no longer this deep longing in me to understand *why* I got my cancer or *why* I kept asking for certain things, like clean scans and *why* I never got them. I had come to finally see that through all of that, He was working around me, and in me, all the time, but just not on my timetable. Now, for the first time, I had come to realize that I was alive by His grace alone and I had the daily reminder of cancer to prove it. More, while I was alive, I still had work to do to honor Him. No longer did I feel the need to know whether or not I would get better or find the answer to the question of whether to hope or to give up. The struggle to trust was the core of the turmoil in me and I had just let go of the chaos that bound me. The more I planned, the more insecure I became and the less glory given to Him. I did not need to feel afraid. I had enlisted the aid of a great and powerful Physician and He alone was going to see this whole thing through with me, in a much better way than I could ever hope to do for myself. Now, I could give up the intense struggle and trust in the process, in the *now*, and in the tapestry God had woven into my being. God had never failed me; I had failed to trust Him. God had never abandoned me. He was with me all along. I had just finally figured out that I could trust Him to take care of me and to love me and Abby and I had the story to prove it. Now, we just needed the medicines to catch up with us, at the place where the storm had stopped and landed us.

...believing, you will receive.

Matthew 21:22

Chapter Nineteen

Recess

I had work to do. More than anything, I had school to complete in order to graduate on time, in December, and this was a *top* priority for me. In addition, I was scheduled for another six day in-patient chemo treatment. I was really quite tired of having my life sound like a medical textbook all the time. So, coupled with my new attitude, I decided to brush off the cobwebs on my dating calendar, fix myself up and try to add a little romance to the story.

I reconnected with a wonderful man that I had casually known in the past. He had no idea how sick I really was and I kept that charade going. I was a master at disguise. I kept our dates short and public and I never let our visits go beyond two hours, in the hopes that I could avoid any *accidents*. He simply made my heart sing and the last thing I wanted to do was stop the music by sharing some sad song and dance about cancer and the effects it was having on me. As much as it scared me to even *think* of adding a relationship to the mix, once I got to know this man better, I lost a great deal of control over that admonition. I had been trying so hard to bury my loneliness with volunteering and fun with my family but always, for me, a key part of the equation was missing. It was so perfect to just go out with a guy I really liked, keep things casual and focus on normal, everyday delights.

As I entered UVA for a round of chemo that would hopefully keep the tiger at bay and get me into transplant, I knew that my new relationship was already in dire straits. Because I had not been honest from the start about my disease, the fact that this endearing man read about it in a newspaper fundraising article about me, did nothing to enhance the seeds of our new relationship. I was so hopeful that we could work things out, once the shocking news of my illness settled with him for a time, but I knew that I could not bring him, like I had done with Chris, into the world, as it existed for me. I had already seen firsthand what that could do to a relationship. I reminded myself that if *we* were in the cards, and in God's plan, then he and I would meet up again, when I got well. Abby helped me to write the hardest *Dear John* letter that I have ever written, giving up a young love, before it ever had the chance to grow. How I wished I could have been writing it to cancer, instead.

Even though I was still fighting the disease, perhaps it was the combination of the approaching Thanksgiving holiday with my family, or just my overwhelming sense of gratitude or simply that I was feeling better—whatever it was—I felt almost celebratory. The idea that I was not alone in my fight and that I had found Jesus, coupled with the overwhelming love of friends and family, made this a special time in my life.

There were *still* problems. I still struggled with the fact that my parents were not together and I still missed having my own time, but I remained optimistic. I enjoyed reconnecting with Bethany Hall, a treatment center where I befriended and counseled women dealing with addictions. I loved seeing my friends and I knew that, without a doubt, my newfound faith was the impetus for my optimism and general feeling of contentment.

The doctors still worked, aggressively, trying not only to address my nerve pain, but also to prepare me for transplant. My medications were adjusted and I began to feel better by taking only methadone for the pain and not the *arsenal* of drugs and steroids and pain patches that I had been previously prescribed. I could literally look at the projected date of transplant on the calendar hanging on the wall and those at the hospital who knew me began to talk in positive terms, too. It was such a relief to know that Abby was ready to begin the process of extracting her cells. Just knowing that we had received the go-ahead with her cells helped me to sleep like a baby at night.

Unfortunately, just after another admission for chemo, I developed another bad case of shingles and I knew that it was probably due to the treatments causing my immune system to fall too low. I was also needing blood transfusions for the first time ever, in my treatment. I passed through these incidents without much *MaDee fanfare*, because I knew that we had a plan. Even if the cancer was not at bay on my upcoming scan, I was still going to admit for another round of chemo and then, proceed directly to transplant. The extra chemo right before I entered transplant would give me a better chance of, once and for all, getting on with my new life.

My doctor and I made a big decision, together. We determined that a hospital in North Carolina was the place where I should receive my transplant. Dr. Douvas and his staff had worked tirelessly for so long on every detail of my case. When he said that he believed Carolina would be the hospital that could admit me the soonest, I trusted him implicitly and readily agreed to the change in direction.

I shaved my head again and I continued to work on my numb feet in physical therapy, pressing through the pain, trying to live my life as fully as I could, given the circumstances. Although I found myself brought to tears about it all, from time to time, something about this relapse was different. I had grown in my faith and I had learned to accept the progress and the setbacks as more in keeping with the plans the Lord had for me. I really tried to make the best of the areas where I had fallen behind when I was so consumed with the pain and with trying to control the outcome of my life. I tried to be a better daughter, a more loving and involved sister and a truer friend. Finally, I was at the end of this interminable wait for transplant and beginning to look at the idea that my prayers just might be answered. I could see the faintest glimmer of light, when I squeezed my eyes and focused, at the end of this long and very dark tunnel. However, on December 4, 2009, as I followed that pinpoint of brightness, I crashed, head first, into another unyielding stone wall. I never even saw it coming.

Play time was over. The tumors had grown, *again*. Just like Humpty Dumpty, I had climbed way up high, on a very tall wall and it was much further down this time, when I fell. The news of disease progression was a complete shock, given that I had been feeling so much better. This kind of setback, for the sixth time in a row, would have brought a grown man to his knees…and that is just where I landed…on mine.

I continued, somehow, through the torrent of disbelief in this news, to grow in my faith. I continued to pray, almost in *blind faith,* believing that I would be healed. I vowed, in the face of such strong and shocking news, to be stronger still. I wanted to be *made better and more complete in His light.* My opponent was a formidable one, but my Leader was stronger still. I felt a renewed sense of determination. I could go another round with Him by my side, in the hospital. I continued to believe that I was headed in the right direction and that I would be *put back together* in no time flat.

The doctors were supportive of my positive attitude. Plans remained in place to send me to transplant, in approximately three week's time and I was going to go, *no matter* what my new scans revealed. Abby was being retested, and the hospital in North Carolina was set up to receive me. It was a complicated scene for me, emotionally, given the approaching holidays, but one that, to me, was as flawless as we could make it, given my history.

The exact treatment plan was three-fold. I would reenter the hospital, locally, to do one more round of chemo and then I would scan, again. If the scan showed good improvement, I would sign on for yet another five day treatment, to keep the beast at bay; the thought being, that three times at bat would be better than two. If, however, my results were less than positive at scan time, then I would leave, immediately, for the hospital in North Carolina to take advantage of the small and closing window of transplant opportunity the new chemo was giving me. Obviously, we all wanted the first option, but no one could predict which door would open for me. This time, headed to transplant, unlike all the other times, there would be no wait for count recovery; the transplant preparation would plummet my counts anyway. Plans were put into place that I would leave, immediately after the scan, for the Tar Heel State, should that be the fork in the road the scan results would reveal.

In the face of such grim news about the tumor's progression, I continued to march, onward, towards the one earthly plan that would save me. How I would get to the goal was an answer none of us knew; but the one thing that we did know, for sure, was that God was in complete control.

I will trust in You.

Psalm 55:23

Chapter Twenty

Cookie Capers And A Parchment Paper

The first of December brought me back into the four blue walls of a hospital room and it was a bit of a dreary and cold start to the season for me, but, from what I could tell of it, looking out the window from my hospital bed, there was a hustle and bustle to the days, typical of holiday preparation. Although it was hard to be hooked up to IVs for almost a week, and restricted to short walks around the ward, I felt good about the decision to get some additional chemo on board.

I wanted more than anything to be out walking among the brightly lit malls and doing some holiday shopping. I had always loved seeing all the decorations and glistening storefront displays and I simply loved the sights and sounds of the season, but I knew that the only way that I was going to have a chance at these pleasures was to get through the hard stuff, first. I had to push myself to make it a joyful time, but so many friends and family visited with me and spent so much time with me that this companionship served to make me feel special and made my admission all that much easier.

I tried to make good use of my time while I was in the hospital, shopping online for gifts for friends and family and signing special Christmas cards I had made, with me and my dog, Mo, on the front. I spent a lot of my time focusing on preparations for the end of my college days. My official, *early* graduation date, December 17, 2009, was only a few short weeks away and nothing filled me with more pride. *I have made it.* Three and one half long years of study, with not one, but *two* degrees. I was so looking forward to a career and I even had the opportunity to speak with a few people about working for the FBI. My degrees in Criminal Justice and Psychology were going to take me far and I was excited to pursue my love of criminal investigation and maybe even addiction counseling, on the side. The world was soon my oyster and I looked forward to turning in my final class work, visiting with my friends, and setting up my final scans before heading off to North Carolina, for more transplant testing. I knew that all these steps were bringing me closer to getting my life right back on target.

Once I was discharged and before the Neulasta shots and the approaching chemo side effects caught up with me—which was inevitable and now something I calendared—I set my sights on getting everything done early, for the upcoming holidays. I made it a point to go out to the shops, even though I bought very little; it was just important for me to experience *the feel of Christmas.* I was crossing out the days of December much like a child does, waiting on Santa. It felt bittersweet to think that I had made it through another grueling year, only to be facing the largest procedure yet.

Preparations for Christmas were in full swing and I actually felt the season's glad tidings release me from my hospital life once I got home and was able to see the family tree and begin to wrap my gifts. In years past, Abby and I made it our tradition to bake cookies...*lots and lots of cookies.* Nannie would buy us dozens upon dozens of bags of flour, pounds and pounds of pure delicious butter and red and green sprinkles from every store. We were the bakers and these were *The Cookie Capers.* We would design our order sheets and spend entire weeks before Christmas baking, packaging and delivering our holiday treats, sometimes late into the night. This year was different, of course, but I still made it a point to bake and deliver handmade treats and home-baked cookies to the staff at the hospital.

My Christmas memories were all such good ones. On the day before Christmas, growing up, we would gather together with my dad's family for dinner and a gift exchange. When we were very small children we would have dinner with my grandma and grandpap and then go to church. When we came home from the service, we would get to unwrap our gifts from Mom and Dad. As we grew older, we developed a bit more patience and we would all go to a matinee of *The Christmas Carol* at the local Blackfriar's Theatre, followed by a wonderful dinner out and then a candlelight service. Seeing everyone in my large and extended family was always something I looked forward to. It was always such a wonderful Christmas Eve in my family and it was, far and away, the time of year that I enjoyed the most.

On Christmas morning, as little ones, we would get up very early and wait for Nannie and Pop to join us for breakfast. Then, they would watch us peer into our stockings and open our gifts, from Santa. The rest of the day we would nap by the fire and leave in the late afternoon for a feast at Nannie's house.

Christmas morning was a special time for me this year, as well. Nannie cooked a big breakfast and I woke up to the smell of eggs and bacon wafting into my room and I heard the sizzle of sausages, frying in the pan. I could hear the coffee pot percolate and smell its rich aroma. There was a glowing fire in the fireplace and holiday music playing in the background. Wandering through the house dressed in my sweats, socks and a three-quarter sleeved tee shirt, the kitchen felt warm and inviting and I sat there for a very long time, sipping coffee and just soaking in the moments. I knew how truly lucky I was to be spending time in a chair at our kitchen table, with my mom, watching Nannie cook. I knew how hard I had fought to make it to this day and, in that moment, I knew that I would never forget one single second of what had brought me to this place. *I have made it to Christmas.* I repeated this thought over to myself, hugging my knees up close to my heart. The only thing that would have made this morning better, was if I could have had the transplant behind me. But, I *knew* that God had a plan for me and all the things that were happening to me were in His order and under His control and not mine.

There was no snow falling that I could see when I opened the back door to let *Mo*, my dog, in from his morning gallivant in the woods. The air was crisp and fresh and the temperature was cold, for Virginia. I remember that the sun was shining down through the trees in the backyard and it looked warmer by degrees than it actually felt. Glancing up at the sun's rays as they filtered through the branches, for a second it almost felt as if church had come to me. I was so thankful. It felt warm inside and I was in no pain. It truly was all the little things... *brown paper packages tied up with string*...that mattered to me.

Once we ate, we set about to open our gifts. I cherished the times that I had had over the last months to shop online for my family and it was with such joy in my heart that I gave everyone their gifts and watched them open them. It meant so much for me to pick just that *special something*, by myself this year, like I had in all the years past. But, I was beginning to get tired now and I started wishing to nap beside Abby, twisting her hair and laughing at Mom's antics or some other farcical story of the day. I wanted to giggle until my eyes closed on the sights and sounds of a family together, at home, on holiday.

This year, while we left it unspoken, I knew that everyone prayed that I would feel good for Christmas and they wanted me to be excited about the day and I *was* excited about Christmas, but, as hard as I tried, it just wasn't the same as it had been before and I think everyone sensed that about me. I used to have such carefree, happy feelings about the holidays and it was infectious. My family rather looked to me for the joy in the house and I was finding it hard to experience those same kinds of carefree, innocent feelings of years past. Although this Christmas was still a happy time for me and I enjoyed all the cozy moments in the little wonderland that we had created, all of us knew that there was a large and looming feeling of uncertainty hanging in the air, like mistletoe. It was all of these thoughts swimming in my head that made it hard for me to hold back the tears, when I opened my gifts. I was overwhelmed with the notion that I had received *the greatest gift of all* this year, that of being alive. There was no need for me to make a list this year, or to even unwrap any gifts. All I could ever want was for this moment to last, forever. So, when I tore the colorfully wrapped paper off of the presents and looked at the gifts that everyone had selected for me, the tears flowed freely from my eyes. There was simply *no way* I was ever going to be able to thank my family for having already given me the greatest gift of all.

How I wished that this blessed day could have been just that simple, like the bicycle under the tree, *wish granted*, there for a little girl to ride forever. I had been home from the hospital for a little over two weeks by the time Christmas rolled around and while I was continuing to feel that sense of accomplishment at having come so far, with my health and with graduation, I was also anxious. The thoughts of being so close to transplant were in one sense, exciting, but they were also very scary. The impending journey sat in the middle of the living room, like the enormous four-legged antelope that it was. No one could deny, even though we tried, the fact that I was scheduled to scan *the very next day*, on December twenty-sixth.

Surrounding the middle of our holiday dinner as we all sat and talked around our plates, I began to feel the anxiety of the looming tests enter the room and get passed to me like a large platter of brussel sprouts. It was such an exciting time, in one sense, to have made it this close to the new year when my transplant could take place, but, none of us knew how the next few weeks would play out and it was, again, all going to be dependent on the tumors and what they were doing inside of me.

Now may the God of hope fill you with all joy and peace in believing.

Romans 15:13

Chapter Twenty-One

Marching Orders

Christmas passed, as it always does, and I felt a bit of relief at having slightly less to do, but also, as the season skirted away, it left me with a bit of longing for the calmness of the holidays. Now, just one day later, it was time to hop back in the saddle and ride off towards treatment. I was growing increasingly concerned about the gaping hole in my chest. What had started out as a dime-sized bump had grown to at least six times that size in a matter of months. Such terrific proportions of tumor stretched my skin to the point that the tumor could not remain in my chest and under my skin. When that kind of thing happens, the only way for the recalcitrant bump to grow, is out, in seeping and less than normal ways. So, when the doctor informed me that my scans the last part of December were in fact *good* and that we would do one more round of chemo here in Virginia, to keep things stable, before heading off to North Carolina, I was actually looking forward to having some help from the nurses with my dressing changes.

While I was in the hospital getting my chemo, Abby had already begun the process of getting her shots and the collecting of her cells. I was amazed at her fortitude. She was a trooper, sitting in a chair watching her blood be siphoned from her, for upwards of six hours, eating twenty Tums to add back in the calcium that was being depleted from her. She endured very painful shots to prepare her blood and body for harvest, all without a speck of complaint. I was over the moon thankful for Abby's selfless and supreme sacrifice.

My transplant was now scheduled, date certain, in January. What a way to ring in the year. There was going to be no need to wait for my counts to recover from this last blast of chemo; the doctors were going to take my blood counts down to zero anyway, so that Abby's cells could do their work. As of the first of January, things were completely on course and like my doctor said, "Nothing can stand in your way now, MaDee."

I was on my way to transplant and the thought of that made me want to sit by the front door, with my suitcases packed to wait for the call. But instead, I went back and forth to the clinic getting platelets and red blood cells, having lunch with friends, and trying to rest, just waiting until I heard that it was time for me to leave.

I felt peace. I knew that I was exactly where I needed to be, doing exactly what I needed to be doing. I had faith that this transplant was going to be the ticket to replenishing all of the gifts the cancer had seemingly taken from me; it was my ticket back to the land of the living. And even if I wasn't going to make it out of transplant, I was going to Heaven; there was no greater place to be. I was a willing participant now and my soul had been set free. I began collecting everything that I could find that was uplifting and encouraging—songs, prayers, mottos and posters—to paste up on my hospital room walls and I placed them in a pile, next to my suitcase. I wanted plenty to do during the months when I would be sequestered after the transplant, so I also packed my scrapbooks, my favorite books and movies and my beloved recipes that I hoped to catalog on my laptop. I waited. Carolina was definitely on my mind the week before I left. I knew that this transplant was my last and best hope.

I was optimistic and scared, all at the same time, worrying about whether we had enough money, and hoping that the stress of my leaving was not going to be too much on my grandparents. I knew that the comings and goings of Mom, Dad and Abby, who were accompanying me and going to stay at various times, were weighing heavily on their work schedules. I knew enough about the treatment that was to come to be frightened out of my mind, for them and for me. But, when the call came in, that a bed was ready for me, I literally danced out the front door, lighter on my feet than I had been since falling ill, two years before. On January 13, 2010, I left my hometown of Virginia, dressed in a light jacket and new blue jeans, with a smile on my face bigger than any I had had in months. *My day* had finally come and as I carried my pillows and my suitcase out to the car, I noticed that the sky was remarkably sunny and it was really quite unseasonably warm, for a day in the middle of winter.

I couldn't help but compare the anticipation I was feeling about the transplant to a child's excitement at leaving for a theme park. I felt such a sense of relief, as if I had climbed the tallest of mountains and could now pitch a tent, sit by the warm fire and smell and feel the crisp new air. As I prayed a silent prayer of thanks, looking up through the oak trees in the front yard, at the beams of light coming down on me through the branches, I felt a lump begin to form in my throat.

I remember saying, as we walked to the car and I stole my place in the driver's seat, "*Guys, this time, I want to drive.*" I knew that this trip was going to be the last time I would ever have to travel by the seat of my pants, with no seatbelt on; because, when I came home, I would be healed; safe and free of the pain that had been my companion for so long. Even though the treatments were going to take me to hell and bring me back again, literally, reborn, I knew that God was with me and that I would no longer be under the umbrella of cancer. I was looking at my final treatment.

I can remember, as Dad sat beside me, reaching over himself to turn on the radio, that we heard James Taylor singing, on one of Mom's favorite stations. As I pulled out of the driveway, I leaned over my shoulder to blow everyone a kiss and then I turned back around, swayed a little bit in my seat and I drove the car away. I hummed along to the words that I knew. *Miss MaDeé Jane Wedge Bomber Nicole Boxler, you sure have seen some fire and some rain.* But, as I turned the car off of the beaten path that led straight for the big highway, I knew that it was now my time to *talk about the things to come.* I was ready to embrace the first day of the rest of my healthy, new life.

...forgetting those things which are behind and reaching forward to those things which are ahead, I press toward the goal for the prize.

Philippians 3:13-14

Chapter Twenty-Two

Rebirth Day

The Transplant Cancer Center at the University of North Carolina Hospital was a flurry of activity when I arrived and was admitted, and they actually served some *not-so-bad* pancakes. I remember thinking how ironic it was that my family was eating pancakes when I was diagnosed and now, here I was, again looking at a stack of them on a plate, waiting on my world to change. I had always had such a difficult time tolerating UVA's hospital food, so being served something so tasty and delicious was a welcome treat, especially since I was going to be eating only their food for the next few months. I had no time to feel scared or apprehensive, or grab another bite to eat again that day, as the pre-transplant schedule for me was full, from morning to night.

The team that was assigned to my case greeted me bright and early that first day and within an hour, my chemo had begun. It was a two drug protocol that would run over the next four days and it was designed to completely wipe my cells and marrow system into oblivion, so that I would be primed to accept Abby's new cells.

All of my organs needed to be checked and many more tubes of blood had to be drawn. Detailed medical histories had to be taken and along with this, I received medications, got lab work done and was scheduled for a liver scan. Sandwiched in between were meetings with a physical therapist, who would keep me active during transplant, a meeting with a nutritionist, who gave me the limited and safe food choices that were permitted and hopefully tolerable and a surgeon who came to see me about the gaping hole in my chest.

On my first day as a new transplant patient, there was no time to nap or to think much about the days that loomed ahead of me. I was finally where I needed to be and I continued to pray for my healing and the strength I would need to muster to face the transplant and its aftermath. My rebirth day, with Abby's healthy new cells, was now set for six days from admission, which in medical jargon was T-6.

There were no secrets kept from me. In meeting after meeting, I was told what to expect with the transplant process. I knew going into this whole scenario that I was not the ideal candidate, because my cancer was not entirely gone, but still, the team was scripted and rather optimistic. I was told that I would need to remain in the hospital for about a month, after which time I would likely go to a step-down unit for a few weeks and then into an apartment on the hospital campus, where I would live out the first one hundred days, post-transplant, with close and constant medical supervision.

I knew that I would feel horrendous once the cells began to take over my marrow, and no one sugar-coated that fact. I was told that I would develop sores throughout my entire digestive system, beginning in my mouth. I could expect the staff not to be surprised if I developed extreme and life-threatening infections. I would lose, temporarily, any ability to fight wayward everyday germs. I knew that I would suffer from many ailments, including a raw esophagus, stomach, mouth and bottom. I was assured that although I would lose a great deal of weight and be unable to eat, I would be fed, via a nasal gastric tube and IVs, the needed nutrients to survive the time when I could not take my own nourishment. I knew that I would have upwards of ten lumens or lines coming into and out of me, going in all directions, giving me the medicines and drugs to keep the pain at bay and to bring me back to health.

I was told that this chemo would kick in and cause my counts to slowly and steadily drop to zero very soon after I received it and that even with the transfusion of Abby's cells, I would not recover the ability to produce cells, for quite some time. It would be during this period that I would have to fight the hardest, physically, medically, chemically and emotionally. Then, if all went well and as planned, sometime around day ten, or +10, after the transplant, I would begin to round the bend and start the upward climb to feeling better and more like myself. With this news in mind, just before the transplant, Mom and I took advantage of every opportunity to be out of my room. I was encouraged to begin a walking program and I enjoyed the walks with her each morning. I loved the staff, who were friendly and helpful and always seemed so knowledgeable and encouraging.

Happy Rebirth Day To Me! My second birthday fell on January 20, 2010. This day was better than reaching double-digits, turning eighteen and then all grown up at twenty-one, rolled up into two bags of plasma. It was a relatively short infusion of Abby's healthy new cells, and to the casual passerby, they probably looked like any other large IV bag full of fluids on the pole. But, once they hit the air, everything smelled like creamed corn and stayed that way for a long time. I had a few reactions to the introduction of something so *foreign* flowing through my veins and into me, but the nurses were easily able to control things. It was a momentous day and I knew that even though Abby was not with me, she felt so happy to be a part of this process. Sometimes, I would steal glances at her picture beside the bed and I just could not believe all that we had been through together. We now shared the bond of common blood and I admired her strength and determination to see me well, probably more than she did mine.

I missed Virginia, almost from the start. A feeling of homesickness hit me hard, but it was mixed with a feeling that I might not ever move back home. I had the idea in my mind that once the transplant was over, I wanted a fresh start, even though I really missed everyone. I had never before been so long without seeing my family and friends, without at least having the option of going to be with them whenever I wanted to. I did not feel like talking on the phone because my throat hurt too much to speak, but I did read the many texts that were sent to me and my messages on the CaringBridge site. It made me miss everyone, all the more.

Nights were the worst. Mom was usually with me, but the darker room, with all the red glowing lights on the IV poles flickering and beaming in all directions and the tangle of lines hooked to me, made sleep elusive. I would watch the clock on the wall, with its big unmistakable black second hand, tick-tick-tick the minutes by, over and over and over again. Time seemed to pass even slower as I watched and it was enough to make me cry, this creeping of the seconds going by, but it honestly physically hurt too much to sob. It was almost impossible to get a good night's sleep, with the constant interruptions from the nurses and my aching throat, tummy and bones.

I would lay in bed, just wishing for daybreak and the next visits from Nannie, my dad, Abby, or our closest friends. Every time the door to my room would open, after breakfast, I would hope to see one of them, all freshly dressed, gowning and gloving up and poking their head in, greeting me with a smile. They carried in their purses and pockets the reminder that life was still going on outside my room and it was just going to be a matter of time before I would join them in it. I looked so forward to the times that they could spend with me, even as horrible as I felt. I knew that having them with me was one good way to pass the time, until Abby's cells could take over.

Mom was great. She epitomized the very essence of strength and at a time like this, there was just no one better than Mom. She would have willingly done anything for me and she performed each task with gusto. She reminded me every day that I was on the *right path* and to just keep on doing what I was doing; that things would get better. A mom's words will always relieve even the most scared and weary soul and I depended on hers.

I would watch Mom try to stuff the knowledge of the things she was seeing and the medical contents of each drawer in the room into her mind. She would mutter, "Packs of petroleum jelly are in the far left drawer; gauze is in the right. I should put my Bible and MaDee's phone on top of the metal dresser where she can reach it." Mom and Abby were the constants in all of this. I knew one of them would be right there for me when I woke up unexpectedly at night and during the day from a nap; always beside me, ready to try to help me combat whatever was irritating me at the time.

Most of Mom's day with me, unless she was reading her Bible, consisted of appeasing me and I knew she was there without even having to open my eyes. No matter how cranky I was feeling, or how mad I would get at her, there she would be, even when I pushed her away; she would just quietly find another spot to rub me, with her strong and loving hands. My lines could be tangled in every which way possible, the machines beeping alarms, and Mom would, as a matter of course, first find a way to calm me before she left the room to find a nurse. Her entire life had become wrapped up in mine, as any mother's life is wrapped up in her children and I knew, without a doubt, even though I never said it much, that she and my sister Abby would go to the ends of the earth to get me better.

Tired does not describe transplant fatigue. I knew that I would feel exhausted as the process wore on, but this was a complete lack of energy to do more than lie in the bed, with the soreness and the sores. I was reminded over and over again by the doctors at each visit that I was doing well and that my numbers were climbing from zero, slowly and consistently, and soon, I would be feeling better and on my way to the step-down unit—perhaps in a week's time. Abby's cells were doing just what they were supposed to be doing inside of me. Even though I could hardly get out of bed, and was on a constant drip of morphine for the pain that dared me to swallow and sleeping twenty-three hours a day, hooked up to fifteen different medications and fluids, I was getting better. My blood counts had doubled and the doctors were cautiously optimistic. Soon, I could *start* to consider myself cured.

Of course, all it would take to set me back was one single germ, imperceptible to the naked eye; one wayward lab report, or my body shocked to the point of rejection of the new cells. If I began to go into defense mode, fighting the very cells meant to heal me, the anti-rejection drugs would kick in. The first one hundred days after the transplant were considered critical. Every single ounce of my physical and emotional countenance for living was geared toward the survival of each and every last one of the smallest of new cells in me. All of my organs, including my heart, liver, kidneys, lungs and even my pancreas, bladder and bowel, in addition to all of my enzymes had been affected and stressed by the transplant, but we hoped not to their breaking point.

I can remember trying to fathom the nurse's words—and they were always the same—as they would look me over and listen to my complaints, "I know it is bad, MaDee, and it's going to get worse, before it gets better; you just need to hang in there." In blind faith, holding a string of floss, I dangled, praying and waiting for those first one hundred days to pass. It had been four days; I had ninety-six more to go, before I could get up and walk out of the hospital and feel the sun shine on my face, again. I wasn't about to give up now; there was still so much living left to do.

For I will restore health to you
And heal you of your wounds...

Jeremiah 30:17

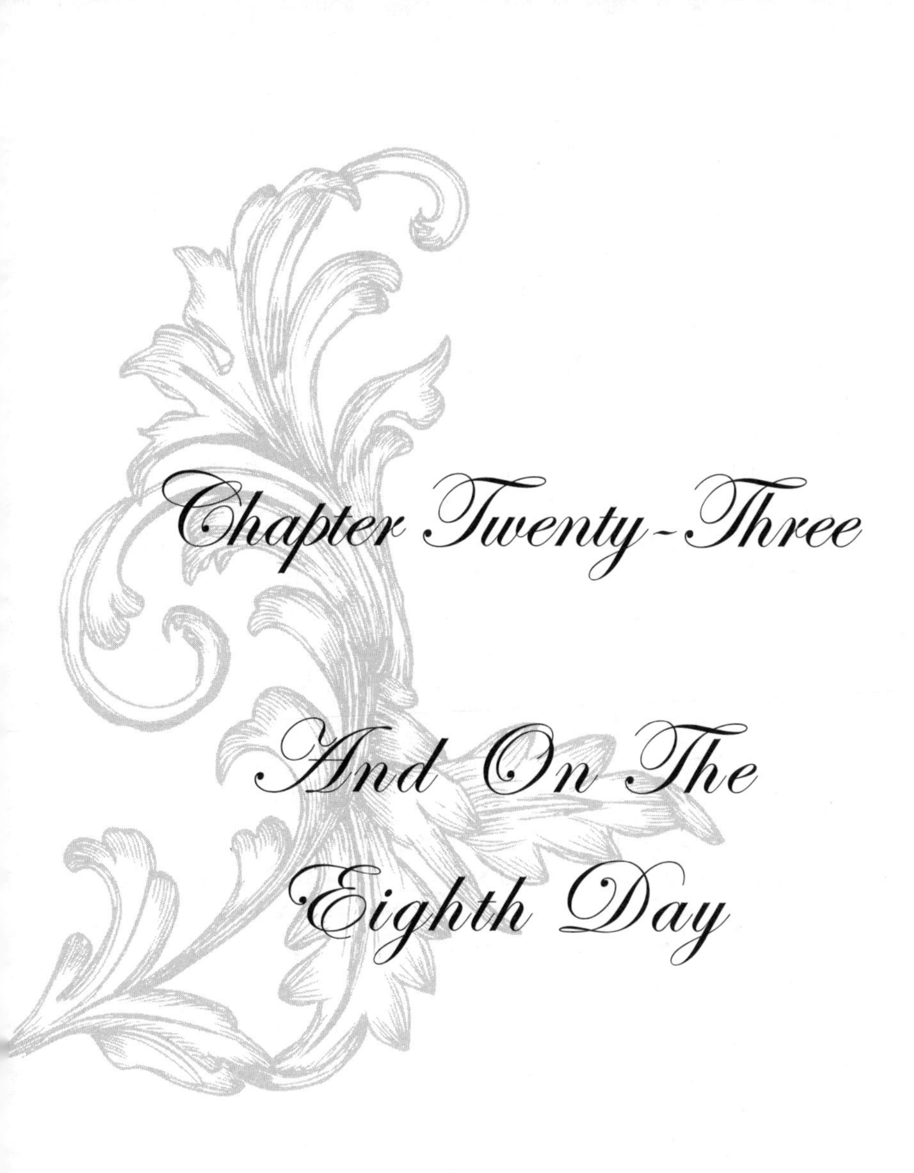

Chapter Twenty-Three

And On The Eighth Day

I woke up from a nap and it was mid-afternoon. I felt horrible. My fingers and my stomach were swollen to the point that I did not recognize them. My hands were so distorted that it looked like I had put an air compressor on them, instead of a basketball and further, that I had forgotten to turn it off. The tightness of the skin on my upper palms made doing more than trying to spread my fingers slightly apart, impossible. I knew that I had been receiving fluids in the many IVs given to me, but something about this swelling was different than I had ever experienced. I asked the nurse if they had started giving me steroids, because I knew that sometimes, that medication would cause mc to retain tons of water.

The worst part of the swelling was the pressure that my enlarged stomach was putting on my chest. My tummy seemed twice its normal size. The only way that I could get a good breath was to be propped up on my pillows and on my left side. I felt like a beach ball, stuck under a lawn chair, ready to pop at any minute.

I remember that my first impulse was to call Abby, but, when Mom got her on the phone I could not speak. Mom laid the phone beside my ear and I let the tears run across my face and into the earpiece. I knew instinctively that something was very wrong. All the alarms had started to go off inside of me. Finally, I mustered up the words to tell my sister, "My body is full of fluid."

Of course, Abby tried to reassure me, speaking to me at a pace and in *that Chrissy tone* she had, that made sure that I would listen to her and calm down, but I could not hear her words. I didn't know what to say or what to think, but I did know that at that moment I felt a terrible sense of being overwhelmed, drowning in my own fluid. For two years I had truly believed that I would never get into this position, in a transplant unit, and more, that I would never have to fight with so much drive and determination to grab a single breath. *I cannot believe this is happening.* Abby told me how fast she could be back, but I couldn't concentrate and I know that I must have sounded panicked. I was. The effort it was taking to breathe was making me extremely agitated and I felt terror at having to gasp for air.

The doctors were notified and after examination, my mom told me that they had surmised that I had several liters of fluid, essentially surrounding my lungs and my abdomen. The idea that I had Dr. Pepper liter-sized bottles of fluid in me that didn't belong there was grotesque. I was put on a breathing mask that gave me oxygen and, as I caught my breath, I listened to everyone talking in the room. I heard the physicians mention something that sounded like an urgent plea for help, from a sinking ship. *SOS. SOS. SOS.*

Now that the oxygen was making me breathe somewhat better, I listened to the conversations in the room more closely. My doctor explained to Mom that, transplant wise, I was doing just fine, which of course was her first concern. My counts were steadily increasing and this was what we thought we most wanted to hear.

But, the doctor continued talking and we learned a whole lot more. I had developed a condition known as VOD, or SOS. The scary, long medical names for my condition were hepatic veno-occulusive disease or sinusoidal obstruction syndrome. VOD, or in the case of transplant patients, SOS, was a complication of the high dose chemotherapy I had received before the transplant started. It was a condition that sometimes occurred in transplant patients when the liver developed blockages. I had all the symptoms. My liver was enlarged. I was swelling and my bilirubin was high. SOS is not as prevalent as it used to be with medical advancements and lesser-toxic chemo, but it was still seen and my doctors were looking at it in me. The fact that I entered transplant without a complete remission was another probable factor for its development and certainly put me at greater risk. We were reassured that SOS was *treatable,* which was all we wanted to hear, but of course, with me as the guinea pig, we were about to learn quite a lot more. Chemo stresses the liver in unbelievable ways, and on the eighth day of my new life, post-transplant, my liver had reached its limit. It was very sick.

The extra fluid was bearing down on my lungs and my heart and I began to require higher levels of oxygen to help me breathe. To make a bad situation much worse, I had to stop all pain medicines, because the drugs were not going to be able to move through my system like they needed to and then be excreted by my liver. It was already too stressed to have to be asked to form waste products from narcotics. This new order resulted in an almost unbearable bone pain to set in, on top of the pain from the swelling and the mucositis, in my raw throat and mouth.

They started me on large amounts of diuretics and I just stayed very still, minute by minute, under all that fluid weight, alternating between dozing for a minute and then in the next few minutes, watching my heartbeat racing and then alternatively slowing down, on the machine's screen above me. I knew enough to know that the nurses were really watching my breathing patterns. I had only one good lung to begin with, the Hodgkin's having already compromised my other lung, so getting one hundred percent saturation into both lungs was not happening. I could see the look of concern on their faces and I knew better than to like what I was seeing.

The doctors reassured me that they would be on top of this and that they would take good care of me. They wanted me to try to rest and I was assured, again, that my transplant numbers were looking good. Still, I couldn't help but notice that their eyes had changed, remarkably, each time they came in to see me. For the first time, I heard mention of the MICU, which meant intensive care. I heard my mom begin asking, in quiet tones, what she was to do with all of my belongings; wondering if she should leave my baby doll Mosey in my bed and my posters on the walls. I am sure it made her feel better to have something she could try to do to help me.

They weren't going to send me to MICU right away. I was still being watched. I thought about all that I had been through; that we had *all* been through. I had seen unbelievable pain in the cancer wards and I had felt a lot of the same. But, absolutely nothing prepared me for the feeling of panic I was having now, or the pained and pathetic expressions of the people standing over my bed. My mom started rubbing me with more force, or so it seemed, and her prayers were being said without noticing who was in the room or what they were telling her might happen. Mom called Abby for me again and I was able to listen to her voice, as she talked to me for what seemed like a long time. She was on her way. I listened to her and then I think I must have dozed off, because when I woke up, she was about to hang up. I managed to whisper into the phone to her…"Love you."

I could sense the room bustling with activity. More hands were attending to me and there were so many nurses in the room. Everyone was doing things to me. I could hear the deeper voices of the doctors. None of this mattered to me now….

My flesh and my heart fail; But God is the strength of my heart and my portion forever.

Psalm 73:26

Chapter Twenty-Four

Peaceful Trinity Shores

Tamara recalls the story of the time when the solitary and simple act of taking a breath became difficult for MaDee. Breathing had become *their* only goal. MaDee had been asleep, but then she sat, bolt upright, in the bed. "It was terrifying for me to watch, and I felt so helpless. . . ." Tamara looks to the side, away from those listening at the table, and bites down hard on the side-edge of her bottom lip.

She sighs, deeply and then she continues. "I remember that she sat up, reached for me and she started to cry. She held out her arms for me." Tamara thinks it was then that she heard the alarms sound on the machines hooked up to her. They began to wail and the doors to her room flew open, hitting the edge of a misplaced chair.

"She tried to speak again, I think, although I don't really remember any words making their way out of her mouth." The act of remembering MaDee this way—of her girl trying to breathe—seemed to stand between Tamara and the words she needed to continue. "I think I might have screamed for the nurses to help her and she looked as if she had that same thought; like she was a child running...you know the look on a child's face, when they are scared and they run for Mom?" Tamara shakes her head slowly and slightly—down, up, down, again—as if she agreed with her own recollection. "I reached for MaDee's arms, then...just when she...when I was over her...I saw her look at me, with tears in her eyes and I heard her whisper to me."

Hold me, Mom. Just hold me.

Tamara knows that she will always remember how MaDee reached for her and said those words, over the rails and the wires and the machines and the sounds of her lungs struggling to breathe.

"MaDee and I took every part of each other that we could hold onto and we stayed like that, for what seemed like forever. I wanted my breath to become hers."

Tamara remembers the nurse leaned behind MaDee in the bed and she pushed the red button on the wall above her. Tamara heard the door open and she saw someone wheel in the red cart that had always been out in the hall, next to MaDee's door. Coming from the speaker in the ceiling, she heard, *Code Blue, Code Blue, Code Blue* and she was asked directly, by one of the nurses, to move to the foot of the bed. They told her that they needed her out of the way, so that they could work.

Tamara remembers more. She "...unwrapped MaDee's arms, one by one and I laid her down. I stood there for a second, watching her and then, I slowly backed away. I was trying to smother in my mouth the idea of screaming the word 'No'."

"I can remember saying, very clearly, to MaDee, as I walked backwards, along the length of her bedside rails, 'I love you, MaDee.' I reached the foot of her bed and I held her feet in my hands. I rubbed them, while the doctor's worked on her, until at last she closed her eyes."

MaDee never woke up after the medical staff rushed into her room and put her to sleep, in order to make her breathe. She was placed on a ventilator and they rushed her to the Medical Intensive Care Unit. Her mom walked beside her feet. MaDee was breathing again, but, she needed constant assistance and more machinery and nursing care than on the transplant wing. The hopes and prayers of the family were that MaDee would be allowed to wake up again, sometime later, after the medicines had had a chance to heal her liver. Her family and her great circle of friends never gave up hope that she would beat this latest setback.

Every effort was made to save MaDee. Drugs were sought from across the country. As the vials of a drug that might heal her liver flew to her from Dallas, Texas, there rained down from the heavens a snowstorm, with ice and snow so fierce that it pelted the tarmacs and froze the wings of airplanes. In short order, pleas for the drug were answered by a hospital nearer to MaDee, that had at least enough medicine to get her though a few more days and very long nights.

MaDee made progress. It was measured in baby steps, forward, backwards and sometimes, when her breathing stalled, they would think that they had lost her. But, always, her team responded and she continued to persevere, against steadily mounting odds, for just under a fortnight. Many efforts were made to stabilize her blood pressure, her heart and her kidneys, all of which were now attempting to deal with the failure of her very sick liver.

Abby knew that MaDee would not want any part of *this*. If she could, she would *just go, leave, get up, get out, be done, be so over it all*, but, when her mind was thinking clearer, she would know that even *this* was all in God's plan and according to His perfect timing. It was not time—yet—for any of them to think that MaDee had been right, when she had told them, *I just think that God has different plans for me.*

MaDee slept on and on, day after day. Sometimes they all thought she must have known that Abby was very close to her face, because the readings on her machines would change, for the better. Her grimace always faded when Abby was with her. There were even times, throughout the days and sometimes nights, when someone sang to her, or soft music played beside her, or Abby read to her, when one or the other of them would remark how *peaceful* MaDee looked.

Finally, there came a day, after MaDee had been unable to speak for a very long time, when the doctors spoke for her. They told the family that MaDee had done all that she could do. She had suffered *such* a setback. Her heart and her lungs were now too fluid-filled and weak. They could not bear the brunt of the impact the liver disease had caused. MaDee had suffered irreparable and multiple organ failure.

Just like that. MaDee was going to have to stop. The machines were set to silent—completely silent—and the room lights were dimmed by the nurses. The ventilator and the strong tape was removed from MaDee's face. Its machinery was then quietly wheeled to a corner of the room. Now, at last, Abby could almost get up in the bed with her. Her mom and her dad could surround her completely. The only sounds left to hear in the room, now that the machines were off, were the sounds of prayer and the quiet whispers and falling tears of those who loved MaDee best.

Tears splashed on MaDee. Everyone stood as close to her as they could and tried to comprehend the incomprehensible; the idea that MaDee was about to leave them. She had worked *so very hard* to stay. MaDee had really only wanted one thing; and everyone around the bed, and just about all across the world had wanted it for her, too. Come to think of it, perhaps MaDee had just reached into her bucket and pulled out her last wish—the one thing she had wanted most of all—but never spoke much about.

Her family knew that they must not try to stop her from leaving, even though the thought of her passing was as lonely as if they were the only people left on the face of the earth. In fact, Abby *pleaded*, as only she could do, for her sister to stay. Abby did not care at that moment if it was God who helped her stay or MaDee who chose to stay; either would be better than to see her Chrissy go.

Abby knew. She knew why Juddy gently tried to unfold her from her sister. She knew what was about to happen and that as much as she wanted her sister to stay, MaDee deserved this leaving. And Abby knew as well that MaDee *surely* needed time alone to go, in her own fashion, in her very own way and all on her own time, just as she had always loved to do. MaDee was getting ready to embark on a journey of the grandest kind, and no one—not any one of them—should *think* of asking her to stay. MaDee had worked as long as she could and she had been as strong as anyone ever could hope for her to be and it was time for her to go.

The nurses wiped away the tears they had taught themselves not to cry, then eased shut the door on the family left in the room. The sun was just beginning to rise somewhere rather far away, over the blue mountain ridges, but in the barely lit room on the fourth floor of the Medical Intensive Care Unit in North Carolina, it seemed as if the night had only just begun. One by one they kissed MaDee and held her hands. Abby laid her hands around MaDee's neck and shoulder and she put her face on her sister's cheek. Everyone wanted MaDee to know that they would hold her until she felt that it was okay to go. They all let MaDee know, that, as much as it hurt, it was okay... to... go. But they still wished that she would choose to stay or that there should be some way they could stop her from leaving.

Time in the room began to feel discordant, as if the sun had forgotten to rise. But everyone knew better than to touch MaDee after a time. MaDee wouldn't like that now. She was well on her way and she would *insist* on being left alone to find her compass. MaDee deserved this trip, in whatever way she could fashion it. MaDee was healed. She had earned her forever.

MaDee Jane Nicole Wedge Bomber Boxler left her baby, Mosey and her big sister, Chrissy on the bed without her. She left her strong and loving parents to somehow go on breathing without her. She led before her special Nannie and her hero, Pop as she made her way to Heaven. MaDee left behind so many who loved her and would miss her greatly.

The hardest thing of all was taking Abby from the bed, when MaDee's spirit left the room. Juddy gently took her in his arms and from MaDee and helped her to stand up. The door to MaDee's room opened and together the family filed out, into the silent hall, allowing the door to quietly close, one final time. MaDee's family walked together, slowly, down the long and empty hallway, not even noticing the closed doors on each side of them. It was a little past four-thirty in the morning, on a cold and rainy February day and it was time to head home. Jesus had MaDee with Him now. Healed. He would lay beside her and rub her back, until the moment when she would wake up and feel Him with her. MaDee would soon open her eyes and realize that she really was, finally, *all better now.*

And, as the family walked away from their angel in the bed, her momma cried, thinking about her baby. And her daddy cried, remembering his Bomber. And, her Abby cried the hardest of all, as Juddy helped her to step away from her Chrissy. And, all around the world, those who knew and loved MaDee would soon hear the news and weep beside them.

And a little child shall lead them.

Isaiah 11:6

Chapter Twenty-Five

Broken Shells

Dear MaDee,

When it rains I see you in your blue striped boots, walking across the campus at Roanoke College. One Sunday at church, a young lady sat in front of me about your size and with curls just like yours. At any minute I thought she was going to turn around and say "Hey, Mom." I talk with you often, sometimes several times a day. I sleep with Mister Bear and Mosey lays on my bed. Several things have happened in the past 16 months that I feel are signs from God letting me know you are alright. As your mom, I worry about that.

Shortly after your trip to Heaven, Molly brought home a dirt-covered sippy cup that she laid right at the back door. I am sure she found it in a neighbor's yard. However, I took it as a sign that you are caring for children in the nursery, in Heaven. You see, when you left, I pictured you in my mind, running into the outstretched arms of Jesus, your curls bouncing. I saw you in the nursery, joyfully rocking babies, telling them stories, and loving all of them. To honor your love for children, The MaDee Project was started. It is a foundation to help other families with children who have cancer.

My first day back at school after your passing was difficult. I knew I had to go, but I didn't want to. The day I went back was windy. I stopped at Nannie's to borrow a stamp. As I was mailing the letter, I looked down and saw a pearly white feather laying by the mailbox. Abby, Lynne, and Nannie had all found feathers that they knew were Heaven sent from you. This was my feather, finally, telling me that you were fine and that I should return to school.

Later on that spring, you made yourself known to me again. I was driving down the road during a rain shower and there appeared a vertical rainbow, not an original arc rainbow. That too, for me, was a sign from you that you were healed and happy.

Abby is doing well. She misses you. On Mother's Day, 2010, she and Jeff surprised us all with the news that they were expecting. You have a nephew, Cy Jefferson Arey. He looks like Jeff and Abby, however, so many of his actions are just like you! He has chubby cheeks, just like you did as a baby. He has your dimple and your smile. We tell Cy stories about you, all the time. There is a beautiful picture of you and Mo in Cy's bedroom. You will always and forever be Cy's number one aunt.

On June 18th, 2011, Steve and I were married. I am very happy. Abby, Jeff, and Nan all gave me their blessing and so did your dad. I know in my heart that you did, too. You were there with us, on my wedding day and you were happy for me. I could feel it.

I know I wasn't a perfect mom, MaDee. We had our heated moments, especially during your middle and high school years. However, I know now that those years were building character traits in both of us that we would need later.

I just finished reading a story written by a dad of a three-year-old that experienced Heaven. I feel much better about being able to see you in my mind now, after reading that book. I can think now about where you are and what you are doing. I had a lot of questions about what it was that I did to cause you to get cancer and why it had to be you so sick, at age 22 and not me, at age 50. However, in my heart I know that God had a plan for you. You touched so many lives, MaDee, and at the young age of 22 you taught me so much about life. Please know that in my heart, you are still very much alive. I will see you again one day, MaDee.

There is a song that expresses how I feel. I hear it all the time and I think of you.

Who You'd Be Today

Sunny days seem to hurt the most.
I wear the pain like a heavy coat.
I feel you everywhere I go.
I see your smile, I see your face,
I hear you laughin' in the rain.
I still can't believe you're gone.

It ain't fair: you died too young,
Like the story that had just begun,
But death tore the pages all away.
God knows how I miss you,
All the hell that I've been through,
Just knowin' no-one could take your place.
An' sometimes I wonder,
Who'd you be today?

Would you see the world? Would you chase your dreams?
Settle down with a family,
I wonder, what would you name your babies?
Some days the sky's so blue,
I feel like I can talk to you,
An' I know it might sound crazy.

It ain't fair: you died too young,
Like the story that had just begun,
But death tore the pages all away.
God knows how I miss you,
All the hell that I've been through,
Just knowin' no-one could take your place.
An' sometimes I wonder,
Who you'd be today?

Today, today, today.
Today, today, today.

Sunny days seem to hurt the most.
I wear the pain like a heavy coat.
The only thing that gives me hope,
Is I know I'll see you again someday.

Someday, someday, someday.

Sung by Kenny Chesney

Who You'd Be Today

Words and Music by William Luther and Aimee Mayo

I kept my promise, MaDee. Abby, your dad, and I, with the help of our friend, Lynne, have completed your Bucket List. We have had your book written. Here it is, MaDee. I hope you like it.

Forever and for always, you are my hero.

Love,

Mom

PS: You were right. Tattoos are addictive. I now have two. I have your cancer ribbon and your signature, from the last card that you ever gave me.

Dear MaDee,

The most difficult year of my life was 2010, when I lost you, and Pop, but, I thank the Lord and Savior for the years I did have with you, both. MaDee Jane, you were one of the dearest and sweetest granddaughters that a grandparent could ever have. As you know, I talk to you every day. I always want you to know how very much I miss you and that someday, you, Pop and I will be together again, in our heavenly home.

I know that you are busy taking care of the all the babies and all the little children in Heaven, but, I still enjoy telling you all about my day and what I have been thinking about. I also know that you honor my wishes, by taking care of your Pop, in Heaven. Hopefully, you have not had to put him back on a "Contract" to make him take care of himself, like you did here, at the house.

The last six months of your life, I so enjoyed having you live with your Pop and me. I will never forget the day I overheard you talking to Pop. You said, "Pop, you expect too much from Nannie…you ask her to do too many things for you; things you could do for yourself. So, I have a Contract for you to sign. This Contract is your promise to me that you will do things for yourself."

MaDee, your sweet, little nephew, Cy, is an angel, sent by God. You would be so very proud of him! He reminds me so much of you, especially when he makes those funny faces and I can see that dimple in his cheek. I call it his "MaDee Dimple."

I cherish the love and the memories I have of you, MaDee Jane. You were always so kind and thoughtful. One of my fondest memories is when you were a toddler. I remember how you would waddle across the yard, from the swimming pool to the swing, where I was sitting. You would hop in my lap and take a nap, while I rocked you, in the sunshine. Once you woke up, you would toddle right back to the pool. You so loved staying with your Nannie and Pop, because you were "the boss" at our house, weren't you? I thank God every single day, for the precious memories I have of you. MaDee Jane, I love you and I miss you, every single day and someday soon, I will be with you and your Pop again.

Love,

Nannie

Dear Chrissy,

I am laying across my bed, listening to the rain on my tin roof. It is a sound I love, although tonight, the sound is almost symbolic of my tears. I miss you, so much. Sometimes, the fact you aren't here just isn't real to me. I said that to Jeff about two weeks ago. "*I just can't believe that she is really gone,*" and then, I got mad at him for not really responding to me. No doubt, he wasn't at all sure *how* to respond to me. Then, we both laughed, through our tears, at the fact that you would probably yell at me for being mean to our Juddy.

Little things can easily make me smile when I think of you, but similarly, it is all the little things that make me sad. I was at a wedding last weekend and I was not crying at the look on the groom's face as he saw his bride, or at how beautiful she looked; I was crying because I would never get to see you as a bride. I knew that I would never get to stand beside you, on your wedding day, like you did on mine. I talked with a friend about my feelings and she said, "MaDee is married to her Maker." I know. I know you are so happy and so at peace and finally, free. I am *so* happy for you, but, selfishly, I just want you here with me.

I hate that Cy won't have you around as he grows up. You would absolutely adore him! He is doing the funniest things now. He reminds me so much of you, with his chubby little cheeks and his fat legs. He has your dimple, on his right cheek. He is just perfect.

There are so many things I want you to know—many of which I'm sure you already do know—you probably feel them, as I do. I remember that on Saturday, February 13th, 2010, while you were in

Intensive Care, I woke up in the hotel room, with an empty, sinking feeling. I was restless and felt, well…sad. I called Mom a thousand times, to check on you. I was ready to be back at the hospital, by your side, reading *The Shack* to you, but Mom and Dad insisted that I rest. I was to be back at 7:00, for the night shift, with Dad. But, there was something inside of me, something that just didn't settle. It was a feeling of indescribable emptiness. I called my friend, and again, I tried to explain how I felt. But, all I could do was cry, despite the fact that you were having a good day. I know, now, that that was the day, or very close to it, that you left this Earth. I felt you go, Chrissy. In the days after that, the grimace on your face was gone. You finally looked peaceful. Mom, Dad and I all used that word—*peaceful*—in our communications with our friend, Lynne, unbeknownst to one another. After a long, tumultuous battle you were finally at peace and able to rest.

I know God healed you, MaDee, in the greatest sense of the word. He gave you what you had prayed for—complete healing. And, although I knew that you were already gone, although I could feel it in my chest, I begged you not to leave me. I pleaded with God, to please, let you stay.

I was able to feel your hand on my neck and face for the longest time. I don't know when I lost the feeling of you, but, it's gone now. When I think of you now though, I see your smile or, I see the funny faces we used to make, like *Kissth Kissth*. I don't see you sick anymore, Chrissy. I hear you laughing or feel us snuggled in your bed and I *love* those memories! I love that this is the way I can remember you, now.

When I look into Cy's big brown eyes, I am completely overwhelmed with love and joy. I am in awe of what God can do. No doubt, I will want to cover his eyes when he is older and he swoons them at me or his newest girlfriend, but, still, I see you in Cy's eyes. I see the miracle of God, in my son.

There are songs that make me think of God best. One song is called *Beautiful Things*. The chorus in the song is:

You make beautiful things
You make beautiful things out of the dust[1]

In my heart, I think of the miracle of Cy's conception, a mere ten days after you left us. Or, his due date, on your birthday. Now, when I look at our beautiful baby boy, with eyes and cheeks just like his aunt and that one dimple that pops, like yours did, with your best, most genuine smile, I *know* that God does in fact give us the most *beautiful things*, from the dust; *your earthly dust.* Don't you dare think that I don't know that you had something to do with Cy coming to us. He is a true miracle and I know that you had a hand in him.

I know you are always watching. Thank you for the dolphins on the beach; I really needed to see them the other day. Sometimes I just have to know that you really do hear me, Chrissy, and that you are still with me. Please know that I love you, more than words in a letter could ever express! I miss you, each and every day and not a single day passes, that you aren't on my mind.

---

1 Song: *Beautiful Things*, Writers: Lisa Gungor, Michael Gungor. *Copyright © 2009 worshiptogether.com* Songs (ASCAP) (adm. at EMICMGPublishing.com) All rights reserved. Used by permission. EMI CMG Percent Control: 100%.

I know that I have purpose in my life. It is up to me to be the best Mommy I can be to Cy. It is my job to make you proud. It is up to me to carry out your legacy and to serve and reach out to others, facing the same battle that we fought, together. I vow to you, MaDee, that I will do my very best to make you proud of me and to do what God has planned for me.

I wish so desperately that I could hug you or touch your face, just one more time or, especially, that I could put Cy in your arms. He is the best little *snuggler*. He has the sweetest little *sleep smell*. You know, I am convinced that you talk to him, sometimes, in his dreams. I ask him, each morning, if you came to see him in the night. While I *hate* that you aren't able to see him grow up, I do know that he has the best, brightest angel, watching over him and that makes me smile.

I don't know how to end this letter. I sat down to write it for your book. We are finishing it for you, Chrissy, just like you wanted. I have so much to say but, I haven't said much, for so long. Now that I am writing to you, I just don't know how to stop.

But I'll do just that, now....

I'll... *stop*....

I love you, my Chrissy....

xo xo

Abby

Chapter Twenty-Six

It's In His Kiss: A Postscript

MaDee wasn't bright yellow the last time she was in a hospital bed. Instead, she was a rather pale hue, like the sun rushing to finish coloring the page, as it came up. They had no name for this shade, in any box of Crayola crayons. The brilliant yellow color that MaDee Jane had been known for all her life, had come the first time, when she was whisked away, sent to a bed, in a strange and faraway place, so that she might learn to pass for pink. It took eleven days back then, before her momma could hold anything more than her baby's feet; this time, it was all of just eight, standing and holding MaDee's pretty painted toes.

Baby MaDee suffered at birth from excessively high bilirubin levels, from a rift between the cells that joined her momma and her daddy. That poor liver of hers got upset again this last time, too, along with the chink between her parents. It certainly did seem to be turning out that MaDee's life had an uncanny way of going in circles, like tricycle tires spinning doughnuts on a driveway. The round and round of MaDee's little wheels didn't seem to leave a mark and no one of us could have ever seen her make every turn, but her whole history was there, when we remembered to go back and look for it.

Tamara can remember MaDee's first tiny breath and she was with MaDee when she took her last. When you see Tamara now, standing at the back door of the kitchen, thinking about that girl of hers, often she has stopped sweeping and she is staring out the window, looking out onto the green pasture fields, watching as the sun playfully rolls over the hay, recalling the time that MaDee had her picture taken there. Tamara seems to have a faraway look in her eyes, as she rubs the folds of her arms with her thumbs. "And you know what?" she will say, if you are there with her to hear. "I always wanted to hold her more." She pauses, but then notices you looking back at her. "In the very last words she ever spoke to me, that sweet child of mine gave me my greatest wish. She looked at me and she asked me to hold her. Now, isn't it just like MaDee to share her finest hour with me?"

Tamara always reminds those of us who ask her to tell us all about MaDee that she hasn't *ever* liked it that MaDee had to leave, or, that sometimes she has a very hard time not thinking about her being gone. But, now, she continues to want to talk about it, as if to get that part straight out of her. "MaDee had it all figured out. She really, really did. Just like she always said, 'There is always tomorrow, right?'" Pondering this last thought, Tamara pauses for a moment, before she bends over to add the dustpan to the dirt, near the brown shag rug, under the kitchen sink. "It's just not ever again going to be a day with my baby girl and I miss her." Breathing in, Tamara rises up and leans against the counter, placing the broom against her legs as if it were a hobby horse. She scratches her head, then starts to sweep a minute longer, before she turns, clears her throat, sighs again deeply and says, "I sure do love her."

The words "*Hold me Mom. Just hold me,*" are, for the family, a culmination of an intense two-year battle, that Mom, Abby, Nannie, Pop and Dad, and all the rest who loved her, waged *with their girl.* Just to think of that now, is *still hard.* Talking to the family and asking them to remember MaDee in that time, can be difficult. Asking them to write a letter to be placed in a book about MaDee—the best friend and the strongest woman they have ever known—is *one* of the hardest things in the world to have to do. But, finding the words to write to MaDee is not what is hard. Abby, Nannie and Tamara have been writing to MaDee for awhile now and it is likely that the thousands of tear-stained words in their journals have only just begun to scratch the surface of their love and relationship. So, the hardest thing, really, in the whole entire world, when you write to MaDee, is not writing to her. Instead, it is as Abby said. The hardest thing of all to do, is to *end* your letter to her.

How does one reach a point in a letter or a book, or, with one song, where we *know* that we have all said enough? Where is it that we have completely explained what she was *really* like? What chapter is all about what she *meant* to us and where can we read about all the things she *could have* become? How do we look up, after a few hundred pages, in a beautifully designed book, close the cover on the last page and mean it when we say, *Yep, that just about covers it?*

The answer to those questions may be that those who love MaDee and who write about that love, are *never* going to reach the point of having said *enough.* So, Abby, you were right. It is exactly as you wrote, in your letter to Chrissy. *We just have to stop.* But, make no mistake about it, this is just a pause, a *dot-dot-dot.* Abby, Mom, Nannie, Juddy and Dad and all the rest of us who love this *spitfire of a girl,* will then go downstairs and for some strange reason, we will smell her lavender lotion or the scent of her hair, and we will pause to think of her. We will find ourselves at the mailbox or on coastal shorelines and we will find white feathers, where there should be none. We will see clouds that look like *M*s or, we will see Pop's rainbow standing right next to hers, after a spring rain and we will pause, in each of these moments and feel her with us, there.

And, if we really want to get MaDee Jane's attention, we might pull through the drive-through lane of Starbucks and up to the window to order. We will smell the brews that mix with the cool air coming from inside and we will again feel the reminder of her. *Yes,* we will say, *one please, and I would like that to be a grande, skinny, half caf, cinnamon dolce latté, one Splenda, with light whip...and, oh, can you please give this book and the drink to the nice looking gentleman in the car behind me? Smile and tell him, MaDee sent it.*

We will all spend the rest of our lives thinking about MaDee, talking about MaDee, loving her, and weaving her into the fabric of our stories, doing all that we can to make sure that her legacy lives on, in the pages of our own books. When it comes to MaDee, we will *never* be able to say enough.

So, as we close this book, for the first time or, for the third time, when we think about MaDee, we can take with us a few final thoughts, just like *you can almost bet* that before MaDee got into Heaven, that beautiful and spirited woman thought about some things, too. We can be sure that MaDee Jane took *very great pains* to think about what she was going to wear to her welcoming party in Heaven. It probably had something to do with ribbons, tall-heeled boots, a suited skirt, a purple scarf, some Pandora *bling* and a leather Coach purse. Grinning from ear to ear, in that way that squished up her nose, squinted up her pretty brown eyes and showed her pearly white teeth, MaDee Jane Nicole Wedge Bomber Boxler probably waltzed her pretty little skirt, and her colorful hair ribbons straight into the arms of Jesus and then, she probably asked Him to tell her where the party was going to be held. Of course, once she remembered her manners, in all that excitement, she would certainly thank Him for having her and she would set about the task of introducing herself.

I am MaDeé, she would look up at Him, smiling and proudly say. *That's Capital-M-a-Capital-D-ee with an accent mark and a* ♥...because she knows by now that Jesus very definitely does love *all the little MaDees of the world.* And perhaps, once we think about her in that way, we will see that MaDee really did get her *happily ever after,* too.

♡ *Greet one another with a holy kiss.* ♡

Romans 16:16

Epilogue

MaDee was seven when her great-grandmother passed away. When her relative's death was explained by the grownups, to MaDee, she responded with all the innocence of a child by saying, "When are we going to the party, Mom?" MaDee thought there ought to be a celebration, because Great Grandma had gone to be with Jesus. MaDee is at that same festive jubilee with Jesus and she was able to attend the festivities, healed of disease and free of pain. This is a promise we can count on.

MaDee was a young lady who, without knowing it, impacted and helped to change the lives of hundreds of people. She was a woman who lived right on the edge of life. She was magical, vibrant, sassy, hardheaded, exalted, uncompromising, stubborn, and heroic. This kind of spirit and attitude is what kept MaDee strong—for her family, her friends and in her battle—against an unrelenting disease. These words describe a daughter, a granddaughter, a sister, a cousin and a friend to many, who made us all better people, because she touched our hearts and our souls with her life and the way she lived it.

Most of us know by now that MaDee had a "*bucket list*." For those of you reading this who are unfamiliar with the term, a bucket list is a statement of the things that we would like to do or to accomplish, before we leave this side of eternity and step into Heaven. While some of us choose not to admit it, each of us probably has a list of some sort that could be described in these terms.

MaDee had three goals in her bucket. She wanted to graduate from college, and she did just that, with a double major, in record time. Secondly,

MaDee wished to attend a Broadway musical show and she traveled to New York. One fine evening, while she was there, she walked through the doors of a famous theatre and realized her wish. MaDee's final goal on her list was to share her story. She made her family promise, that one day, if she was unable to complete it, they would see to it that the story she had started would be written. This is her story. It has been told.

All of us are writing the story of our lives, just like MaDee did. And, like MaDee, one day, we will pass from this life on Earth to the Other Shore of Eternity. But, while we are alive, God is always creating moments for us to share and stories for us to tell. Life is never meant to be lived in isolation, but in fellowship and in *story* with other people.

In the beginning, our Creator gives each of us an instrument to help us write the story of our lives. Our story is written in the recesses of our heart and the pen is the set of full experiences that make up our life. Each chapter may look different to each individual. In our stories there might be chapters filled with drama and pain; some chapters may be riddled with comedy and laughter and other chapters may be filled to the brim of the page with love and romance, with a smattering of tall adventure and gripping suspense for good measure.

The truth is, all of us have a story to share and MaDee is just one part of our complete story. But, every time we think of her, see a picture of her, read about her in this book or further the goals of The MaDee Project, we are honoring MaDee and continuing to write her story and, more importantly, we are connecting her to our very own pages. To everyone who nurses a sick child or infirm family member and to all of you who learn, from her example, to dance in the midst of life's storms, you are as much a part of MaDee's story, as if she had handpicked you, herself. In some way or another we are all written into the chapters of each other's lives and it is an honor and a privilege for me to be a character in MaDee's story. I am humbled to have shared in the life of MaDee Nicole Boxler, who will live on, forevermore, in our hearts and in our minds. MaDee Nicole Boxler left her handprint on my life and she challenged me to always be reminded that God's goodness is alive and well, and, at work in each of us, every day. I hope she will do the same for you.

MaDee's story never ends, even after she sheds her physical body, because life is the story you write as you live it each day. You and I still have the opportunity to continue to write our own story, but also, to continue to write a verse or two in MaDee's story and then, share it. This book, *Dancing in the Rain* and The MaDee Project are just two of the ways we have let it be known that this awe-inspiring woman left her handprint on our lives, forever.

I believe that we can see how God's goodness is at work in each of us, by reading MaDee's story. If we believe that we were all created in the image of our God then we can see pieces of God's character in the life of MaDee. Though there are no clear answers for what happened to her, God lets us know, *in His story,* that His heart breaks too and that He grieves, alongside of us. In that same breath, He lets us know that His love for us is beyond our comprehension. He will comfort us, guide us and love us, even as we wrestle with the anger of a wayward cell, the questions about the unfairness of relapse and the grief of losing one so very young. God's love always wins and through His love each of us can and will find the strength to rise above the pain, suffering and sorrow in each of our stories. God lives in us and He has made available to us the strength to live our lives to the fullest.

I challenge you to finish writing the story of your life with God, and with MaDee Boxler in it. Do not live out your story alone. God has given you the Guide. Whenever the rains fall, however unexpectedly the drops pelt against you—whatever the words on the page you find yourself penning—God will be with you, even unto the end of time. You and I are part of MaDee's story, forever. Pass on her pen. Begin to write the page:

I once knew a person and her name was MaDee, and my, how she loved the Lord.

Continue to write and continue, always, to pray.

Blessings,

Jeffrey Griffith, Pastor
Community Fellowship
Church of the Nazarene
Waynesboro, Virginia

"And whatever things you ask in prayer, believing, you will receive."
Matthew 21:22 NKJV

The MaDee Project is a non profit foundation that continues MaDee's legacy of caring for the children into the homes of our pediatric patients in our community by providing financial assistance and hope to these families facing pediatric cancer treatments.

To join us in our mission or to learn more visit us on the web at:
www.themadeeproject.com

or email us at
office@themadeeproject.com

Net proceeds from the sale of this book will support the construction of the new Battle Building at University of Virginia's Children's Hospital. This new outpatient center will consolidate pediatric services in a convenient, cheerful and family-centered care setting with an entire floor dedicated to cancer services for kids. The MaDee Project hopes to raise sufficient funds to name a room in the Infusion Center in memory of MaDee.

Additional copies of ***Dancing in the Rain*** are available on our website's online store.

www.themadeeproject.com

About The Author

KIMBERLY FOWLER is first and foremost a mom and more than anything a Christian. She is an author, teacher and former paralegal, who holds a law degree from Pepperdine University, School of Law. She lives in Southern California with her two sons, Ryan and Evan. In her words, the ideal spot would be on a deck, brimming with geraniums, hibiscus and a tomato plant, with a book to write and an astounding view of the sea. To contact Kimberly or to learn more about MaDee Boxler or the work of the Project, please visit them at:

www.kimberly-fowler.com
or
www.themadeeproject.com